[redacted]

EVIDENCE FOR THE MINOAN LANGUAGE

EVIDENCE FOR THE MINOAN LANGUAGE

by

CYRUS H. GORDON

•

VENTNOR PUBLISHERS
VENTNOR, N. J.

PRINTED IN THE UNITED STATES OF AMERICA
PRESS OF Maurice Jacobs, INC.
1010 ARCH STREET, PHILADELPHIA, PA. 19107

IN MEMORIAM

MINNIE AND PHILIP SAGOFF

FOREWORD

This monograph aims at providing qualified scholars with all the evidence they need for understanding the Northwest Semitic character of Minoan.

One of several valid ways of summarizing the thesis is as follows: (1) the decipherment of Mycenaean makes it possible to pronounce most of the Minoan syllabary (§114); (2) virtual bilinguals provide opening wedges for identifying the Minoan language (§§115–116); (3) contextual evidence (§§117–123) yields Northwest Semitic readings known from comparable Phoenician inscriptions (§§120–124); (4) Eteocretan is a continuation of Minoan (§124); (5) the Northwest Semitic character of Minoan-Eteocretan is confirmed by the Dreros bilinguals (§§19–31).

The decipherment is validated by the established results; it is in no way shaken by inconclusive or even mistaken details beyond those established results. Northwest Semitic is the only possible classification of a language that goes with Hebrew-Phoenician-Ugaritic in expressing "the, this, his, for, and, all, it will be, he gave, I gave, mother, people, friend, companion, city," three numerals, a variety of nouns for common objects and commodities in daily life, etc. (§§113, 126). The morphology is of course good Semitic. Beyond our definitive results, are tentative suggestions not meant to be final but rather to serve as stepping stones for scholars who will enlarge and refine the decipherment. Chapter XIV on the Phaistos Disc is especially subject to correction, for the interpretation of the Disc is lagging by several years behind our decipherment of Linear A Minoan. And yet, it is necessary to consider such ancillary topics as the Disc and Eteocypriote (§§3–18) because they are part of Minoica. Eventually still other inscriptions will have to be brought into the discussion: notably the Cypro-Minoan tablets from Enkomi (§18).

I hope many readers, after digesting this monograph, will turn to the corpus of Minoan and Eteocretan texts to make fresh contributions of their own. In the near future, the publication of the newly found Minoan tablets from Kato Zakro will be a welcome addition to the corpus.

The appearance of this monograph was made possible through a generous gift of my friend Helen Sagoff Slosberg in memory of her beloved parents, the late Minnie and Philip Sagoff of Cambridge (Mass.), who transmitted to her their reverence for Hebraic learning. I am also beholden to President A. L. Sachar and Dean Peter Diamandopoulos of Brandeis University for a research grant that helped bring this book to the light of day.

Brandeis University
Waltham, Massachusetts 02154

Cyrus H. Gordon

10 February 1966

TABLE OF CONTENTS

PLATES

EVIDENCE FOR THE MINOAN LANGUAGE

I. INTRODUCTION

1. A comparative study of Ugaritic, Greek and Hebrew literatures points to a single culture that permeated the East Mediterranean throughout the second millennium B.C.[1] Inland, other cultures predominated, such as the Egyptian in Upper Egypt, the Hittite in Anatolia, the Assyro-Babylonian in Mesopotamia, etc. But near the waters of the East Mediterranean (whether on the shores of Africa, Asia, Europe or the islands) a single element dominated the cultural and economic life and possessed enough naval strength to maintain its supremacy. Until the fall of Knossos to the Mycenaean Greeks (sometime between 1400 and 1200 B.C.)[2] that thalassocracy was centered on Crete. As the Greeks were gaining possession of the island, the pre-Greek thalassocrats, whom we call the Minoans, had to seek other bases in safer areas. It is for this reason that sometime after 1400 B.C. there is evidence of the renewed spread of Minoan influence from Crete all over the Mediterranean. It is after 1400 B.C. that Ugaritic literature suddenly appears, referring to Caphtor (=Crete) as the home of the god of arts and crafts. That god (Kothar-wa-Khasis) has a pure Semitic name, indicating that Caphtor had been the artistic center of the linguistic, cultural and religious sphere to which Ugarit belonged. Prior to 1400 B.C. the Minoan hide-shaped ingots come mostly from Crete; thereafter they are found at many points, from Anatolia to Sardinia, reflecting the diffusion of the Minoans after that date.[3]

[1] C. H. Gordon, *Common Background of Greek and Hebrew Civilizations*, Norton, New York, 1965. Arnold Toynbee, in his review of the first edition of this book, appraised the situation with clarity and verve (*London Observer*, 16 Dec. 1962). Note also the estimate of R. Arrillaga Torrens, *Memoria de un viaje en el tiempo*, Editorial Club de la Prensa, San Juan de Puerto Rico, 1963, pp. 102–105. See now especially M. Astour, *Hellenosemitica*, Brill, Leiden, 1965.

[2] Any reduction in the chronology of ancient Western Asia or Egypt must also be applicable to Crete because of the synchronisms. In general I favor the lower dates because most of the dark ages tend to be inflated. (F. Matz, however, opposes the reduction in the chronology; see his *Cambridge Ancient History* pamphlet *Minoan Civilization: Maturity and Zenith*, Cambridge University Press, Cambridge, 1962, pp. 39–40.) When I give the higher dates (such as 1400, below), it is partly because they are conventional. As long as the synchronisms are kept in mind, our historic conclusions are not affected by whether we follow a higher or lower chronology.

[3] Later, at the beginning of the twelfth century B.C., the Sea People attacked the shores of the entire Levant. They included the wave of Philistines that put Palestine under Philistine domination until David's victories around 1000 B.C. It is interesting to note that the Philistines worship a Semitic god (Dagon), bear Canaanite names (like Abimelech) and are linguistically Semitized so that they never need interpreters in conversing with the Hebrews, because they spoke Canaanite in their Aegean homeland before migrating to Palestine.

2. The descendants of the Minoans lingered on in their old haunts as dwindling communities until they were eventually displaced by the Greeks. But on Crete and Cyprus they retained a knowledge of their native syllabary into Hellenistic times (§§3–5, 45). Moreover on both islands bilinguals have been discovered in which the Greek version provides the key to the old pre-Greek tongue.

II. ETEOCYPRIOTE

3. We start our examination of the evidence with the Greco-Eteocypriote bilingual from Amathus (Plate I). This text[4] is inscribed on a black marble slab, found in 1914 on the acropolis of Amathus, east of Limassol, Cyprus. The syllabic Eteocypriote is so much longer than the Greek text, that the latter can only be an abbreviated version, lacking even the verb that tells what the city (nominative) did to honor Ariston (accusative).

4. The Eteocypriote syllabary consists of signs for open syllables. Each Eteocypriote series of stops is covered by a single set of signs so that the labials (*p*, *b*), dentals (*t*, *d*, *ṭ*) and palatals (*k*, *g*, *q*) are not orthographically distinguished as to surd, sonant and emphatic. A single set of signs covers all the sibilants, so that *s*-signs may call for normalizations with *z*. The so-called pure vowel signs (*a*, *e*, *i*, *o*, *u*) actually call for a laryngeal before the vowel; so that *a*, for example, may stand for *'a*, *ha*,[5] *ḥa* or *ʿa*. A consonantal series has five inherent vowels; thus there are five signs for the dental stops: *ta*, *te*, *ti*, *to*, *tu*. Vocalic and consonantal length are not indicated in the spelling.

5. Since the two main languages of Hellenistic Cyprus were Greek and Phoenician, we shall probe the Eteocypriote version of the Amathus bilingual to see whether it is Northwest Semitic akin to Phoenician. The Eteocypriote text runs thus:

1) *a-na . ma-to-ri . u-mi-e-s[a]-i mu-ku-la-i la-sa-na . a-ri-si-to-no-se a-ra-to-wa-na-ka-so-ko-o-se*
2) *ke-ra-ke-re-tu-lo-se . ta-ka-na-[?-?]-so-ti . a-lo . ka-i-li-po-ti*

6. The Greek epitome runs thus:

1) Η ΠΟΛΙΣ Η ΑΜΑΘΟΥΣΙΩΝ ΑΡΙΣΤΩΝΑ
2) ΑΡΙΣΤΩΝΑΚΤΟΣ ΕΥΠΑΤΡΙΔΗΝ

"The city of the Amathusians (has honored) the noble Ariston (son) of Aristonax." The text does not tell us how the city honored him but according to Masson, the monument has markings indicating that a statue (presumably of Ariston) was originally mounted over the inscribed stone.

7. The equation *a-na . ma-to-ri* = ἡ πόλις shows that *a-na* = *hānā* "the, this" as in Syro-Aramaic and Ugaritic, and that *ma-to-ri*[6] = Hebrew מָדוֹר (cf. Aramaic מְדָר) "a dwelling, habitation."

[4] Republished by O. Masson, *Inscriptions Chypriotes Syllabiques*, Éditions E. de Boccard, Paris, 1961, pp. 206–209.

[5] Greek orthography reflects this polyphony for α can stand for ἀ (*'a*) or ἁ (*ha*).

[6] The form may be grammatically plural ("these dwellings = this city") with the m. pl. suffix *-ê* found in certain Akkadian and Aramaic dialects; in Aramaic, the form we refer to is not the construct but the emphatic m. pl. in *-ê*.

8. Both *u-mi-e-s[a]-i* and *mu-ku-la-i* look like toponyms with the gentilic ending *-â'ī*.[7] *U-mi-e-s[a]* could be the *qutêl* (<*qutayl*) diminutive of "Amath(us)." There follows the gentilic of Mukul (מכל *mkl* in Phoenician), usually cited in the form "Mikal" (cf. 'Αμύκλαι).

9. *La-sa-na* = Phoenician לזן and Old Aramaic לזנה *lzn*(*h*); i.e., Northwest Semitic *la* = ל "for" + *zana* = זנה "this" (m. sg.); "for this one" anticipates the name of the noble who is honored in the text.

10. *A-ri-si-to-no-se* = 'Αρίστωνα with the suffix *-o-se* = the Cypriote Phoenician demonstrative pronoun אז *'oz* "this" used enclitically.

11. The discrepancy between *a-ra-to-wa-na-ka-so*(*-ko-o-se*) and Aristowanax is discussed by Masson, p. 207; 'Αρτοϝάναξ and 'Αριστῶναξ are interchangeable. The ending *ko-o-se* = Hebrew כָּזֶה "this"; for the prefix כ with the demonstrative pronoun with no change in meaning, note לעת כזאת (Esther 4:14) "for a time like this" = "for this time," and כאלה תעשו (Numbers 28:24) "like these things shall ye do" = תעשו את־אלה (verse 23) "ye shall do these things."

12. Perhaps *ke-ra-ke-re-tu-lo-se* designates a native Semitic name for Amathus, beginning with *krak* = כרך "city" and ending with אז *'oz* "this." At the same time, it could conceivably correspond to εὐπατρίδην.

13. The verb may be contained in *ta-ka-na-*[*?-?*]; for תקן *tqn* means "to set up, restore"; the ending *so-ti* could stand for a feminine object = *zôti* (Hebrew זאת *z't*) "this (sc., monument)."

14. *A-lo* corresponds well to Hebrew עליו *ʿālāw* "over him." This gives good sense, for the monument was erected over his grave.

15. The concluding phrase, *ka-i-li-po-ti*, may be analyzed tentatively thus: *ka-* (as in Hebrew, Arabic, etc.) is the Semitic preposition "like, as"; the rest is a noun known from Ugaritic *ilib* "a memorial monument" with the gentive fem. sg. suffix *-oti*.[8]

16. The Eteocypriote version would thus mean: "The Amathus-Mukul community, for this Ariston (son of) this Artowanax — yea this City-of-X, erected(?) this over him as a memorial monument."

17. If we sum up the evidence of the certain and the highly probable readings (and omit entirely the less probable ones), Eteocypriote emerges as Northwest Semitic in vocabulary, morphology and syntax: The m. sg. suffixed personal pronoun is *-ō* in *a-lo* "over him." The m. sg. independent demonstrative pronoun is *sa-na* (זנה) "this" and the enclitic m. sg. form is *-o-se* (אז) "this"; the two demon-

[7] Probably we are dealing with the m. pl. of this gentilic; namely, *-â'ê*. For examples, note the Qre of כַּשְׂדָּיֵא (Daniel 5:7) "Chaldeans" and the whole series in Ezra 4:9: אֲפָרְסָיֵא אַרְכְּוָיֵ בָבְלָיֵא שׁוּשַׁנְכָיֵא and עֵלְמָיֵא "Persians, Erechites, Babylonians, Susians" and "Elamites" (with *-â'ê* > *-âyê*).

[8] From original *-ati* (§152).

stratives are used simultaneously in *sa-na a-ri-si-to-no-se* "this Ariston."[9] The definite article "the" is *a-na* (pronounced like Syriac *hânā*=Ugaritic *hn*), so that *a-na . ma-to-ri* corresponds to ἡ πόλις. If we compare the m. noun *ma-to-ri* "town" with the f. noun *i-li-po-ti* "memorial monument," the suffix of the f. noun appears as *-ot* (the Phoenician pronunciation of what appears in Hebrew as *-āt*). The gentilic suffix *-â'ī* occurs in *u-mi-e-s[a]-i* and *mu-ku-la-i*. Three prepositions are attested: *ka*=כ "like, as," *la*=ל "for," *ᶜal*=על "upon, over."

18. Some of the other Eteocypriote texts provide some details that tend to confirm the Northwest Semitic character of the language.[10] A different class of Phoenician texts from Cyprus is written in the regular Phoenician alphabet.[11] However, before the introduction of the alphabet to Cyprus, the use of the old syllabary is attested by the Cypro-Minoan texts from Enkomi in the Late Bronze Age.[12] This Cypro-Minoan tradition was quite strong because both Greeks and Semites continued to use the Cypriote syllabary side by side with the Greek and Phoenician alphabets into Hellenistic times.

[9] For the double demonstrative with personal names, cf. Aramaic להדין פרוכדד דנן "for this Farrukdad" (*Archiv Orientální* 6, 1934, pp. 328:329, lines 13–14).

[10] C. H. Gordon, "The Mediterranean Factor in the Old Testament," *Supplements to Vetus Testamentum* 9, 1963, pp. 29–31. Note the personal name *pu-nu-to-so* (which can also be read *bu-nu-do-šo*)=בן חדש *bn-ḥdš* "Son-of-the-New-Moon": a man's name found on five Phoenician inscriptions including two from Cyprus; and *ta-we-ta-re-se* (which can also be read *da-we-da-re-še*)= דוד ראש "David-is-Chief" (*da-we-da* "David" occurs four times in Minoan; see §§133, 163; for the vocalization of ראש, cf. Ugaritic *riš* "head" and Hebrew רֵאשִׁית "beginning" as in Genesis 1:1).

[11] G. A. Cooke, *A Text-book of North-Semitic Inscriptions*, Clarendon Press, Oxford, 1903, see texts 11–30; and Masson, *op. cit.*, p. 429, for the indexed references. The standard work covering the Phoenician inscriptions is now H. Donner and W. Röllig, *Kanaanäische und aramäische Inschriften* I–III, Harrassowitz, Wiesbaden, 1962–64; the texts from Cyprus are numbers 30–43.

[12] P. Meriggi, "I Primi Testi Ciprominoici e l'Eteociprio," reprinted from *Athenaeum* 35, 1956, pp. 1–38; P. Dikaios, "The Context of the Enkomi Tablets," *Kadmos* 2, 1963, pp. 39–52.

III. THE ETEOCRETAN TEXTS

19. Two bilinguals from Dreros (Plate II) give the Eteocretan text first and then the Greek version, suggesting that the principal language of the town was Eteocretan although the Greek minority was large enough to evoke bilingual inscriptions.

20. The Eteocretan section of the First Dreros Bilingual[13] has word dividers and runs retrograde (i.e., from right to left) throughout, in the Northwest Semitic tradition:[14]

1)]Ị̣PMAϜ . ET . ΙΣΑΛΑΒΡ ΕΤ ΚΟΜΝ̣

2)]Δ . ΜΕΝ . ΙΝΑΙ . ΙΣΑΛΥΡΙΑ . ΛΜΟ

21. The Greek version lacks word dividers, and is boustrophedon starting retrograde like most of the early Greek texts from Crete:

3)]Σ ΤΟΝ ΤΥΡΟΝ Μ[ΥΝ]Α ΤΟ ΑΟΙ ΕϜΑΔ

4) Ε ΤΥΡΟ[ ] Μ̣Υ̣ΝΑ Τ̣Ο Α[ΟΙ]Ν[ ]

5) [ΤΑΙ] ΜΑΤΡΙ ΤΑΙ Α[ϜΤΟ]

22. The Eteocretan is better engraved than the Greek and its readings are clear. The final word in the Eteocretan is ΛΜΟ corresponding to]ΜΑΤΡΙ ΤΑΙ Α[. Since ΜΑΤΡΙ can only be the dative for "mother," the Eteocretan ΛΜΟ is the equivalent of Hebrew לאמו[15] *l'immō* "for his mother." The Eteocretan pronoun "his" points to the restoration [ΤΑΙ] ΜΑΤΡΙ ΤΑΙ Α[ϜΤΟ] = *τῇ μητρὶ τῇ αὐτοῦ*.

23. In my preliminary publication[16] of this text I shied away from taking ΤΟΝ ΤΥΡΟΝ in its obvious classical meaning of "the cheese" (accusative). However, the offering of cheese appears in Linear B[17] and it is therefore not out of the question for it to crop up at Dreros. The accusative ΤΟΝ ΤΥΡΟΝ would then correspond to ΕΤ ΚΟΜΝ in the Eteocretan, for ΕΤ is the sign of the definite accusative (= את *'et* in Hebrew and sometimes in Phoenician). ΚΟΜΝ (see §§40, 44) can be explained as a form of Semitic *gbn* "cheese" (Hebrew גבינה, Arabic جُبْن) with the labial stop *b* becoming the labial nasal *m* through partial assimilation to the nasal *n*.

[13] H. van Effenterre, "Une Bilingue Étéocrétoise?," *Revue de Philologie* 20, 1946, pp. 131–138. I am indebted to Professor van Effenterre for photographs of the Dreros bilinguals.

[14] A dot beneath a Greek letter means that the letter is not completely preserved. A dot between words indicates a word-divider on the original stone; otherwise the words are run together by the scribe and have been divided by the present writer.

[15] For the absence of the א in sandhi, cf. the Ugaritic name *išrmy* "Ishtar-is-my-Mother" = syllabic *iš-tar-um-mi-ya*; see p. 543 of UT (C. H. Gordon, *Ugaritic Textbook*, Pontifical Biblical Institute, Rome, 1965).

[16] C. H. Gordon, "The Dreros Bilingual," *Journal of Semitic Studies* 8, 1963, pp. 76–79.

[17] M. Ventris and J. Chadwick, *Documents in Mycenaean Greek*, Cambridge University Press, Cambridge, 1956, pp. 282–283, for *τυρός* "cheese" offered to Poseidon.

24. The repetition of ΜΥΝΑ ΤΟ ΑΟΙ, corresponds to the repetition of ΙΣΑΛ- in ΙΣΑΛΑΒΡ and ΙΣΑΛΥΡΙΑ; the Greek and the two Eteocretan expressions would mean “one (f.) to another (m.).” There are difficulties that confront us but yet the bilingual evidence makes a number of correspondences clear. We take ΙΣΑΛΑΒΡ to stand for what would appear in Hebrew as אשה לחבר *’iššā lᵉḥābēr*, literally “woman to companion”; and its parallel ΙΣΑΛΥΡΙΑ, as אשה לרע *’iššā lᵉrêaᶜ* “woman to friend.” That we are dealing with “woman” rather than ΙΣ = איש = *’îš* “man” is indicated by f. ΜΥΝΑ (for classical *μονή*; note also Homeric *μοῦνος* for *μόνος*). That this f. is followed by a dative m. is supported by ΤΟ ΑΟΙ; the omission of the iota from the m. dative article, but not from the noun, is matched in a text reproduced in C. D. Buck, *Greek Dialects*, Chicago, 1955, pp. 35, 213 (text 24). The noun meaning “other,” represented by the single letter Α, is elusive. If it were followed by Λ, we would have the normal reading of ΑΛΟΙ (archaic for classical ἄλλῳ); but there is no room for the Λ.[18]

25. The verb ΕϜΑΔΕ “decreed” should correspond to the Eteocretan]Ι̣ΡΜΑϜ.

26. Eteocretan ΜΕΝ looks like the West Semitic preposition “from” (e.g., *men* “from” in Syriac = Hebrew מן *min*); and ΙΝΑΙ, like Hebrew עיני *ᶜênê* “the eyes (of)”. If this is correct, ΜΕΝ ΙΝΑΙ ΙΣΑΛΥΡΙΑ would mean “from the presence of one another.”

27. The First Dreros Bilingual provides Greek evidence that establishes the close Eteocretan correspondents of Hebrew/Phoenician ל “to,” ו “his,” אם “mother” and the accusative indicator את. Even if we set aside the other Eteocretan readings, these four would fix the Dreros dialect as Northwest Semitic.

28. Wm. A. McDonald has republished the Second Eteocretan-Greek Bilingual from Dreros in *Hesperia* 25, 1956, pp. 69–72 and pl. 27. The end of the Eteocretan version is preserved:]Σ . ΤΥΗ̣Ρ ΜΗΡ ΙΗΙΑ.

29. The Greek version is preserved at both the beginning and end, with but little broken away from the middle: ΟΜΟΝΤΑΙ ΔΑΠΕΡ ΕΝ ΟΡΚΙΟΙΣΙ . Α[ ] ΚΑΘΑΡΟΝ ΓΕΝΟΙΤΟ.

30. The text has to do with avoiding the wrath of the gods in whose names unfulfilled vows had been made. The goal of the text is purification. The divider in both versions enables us to equate ΤΥΗ̣Ρ ΜΗΡ ΙΗΙΑ = Α[ ]ΚΑΘΑΡΟΝ ΓΕΝΟΙΤΟ. What is clear is that Eteocretan ΙΗΙΑ corresponds to Greek *γένοιτο* “let him be.” The Semitic ΙΗΙΑ (in Hebrew יהיה *yhyh*)[19] by itself means “he will

[18] These epichoric texts do not reflect the standardization of any Greek or Semitic academy. Their dialects and orthographies were local and must not be expected to comply with the classical rules of Attic Greek or Masoretic Hebrew.

[19] For initial *y*->’-, cf. יצחק = ΙΣΑΑΚ “Isaac,” ישראל = ΙΣΡΑΗΛ “Israel,” etc.; for standard Hebrew *e* (as in יִהְיֶה *yihye*) = Α, cf. חַרְנֶפֶר (1 Chronicles 7:36) = ΑΡΝΑΦΑΡ, אֶזְבָּי (1 Chronicles 11:37) = ΑΖΟΒΑΙ, etc. In the supralinear Babylonian Masorah, short *a* and *e* fall together. In the early epichoric texts, Η is regularly consonantal; only in the later texts does it become vocalic.

be" (indicative) though it is rendered by an optative in Greek. The nuance in the Greek may be provided by a Semitic adverb such as MHP = Hebrew מהר *mahēr*. The latter means "quickly" and, if correct, might possibly point to the restoration A[IΠΣA] (= Homeric αἶψα "quickly"). ΚΑΘΑΡΟΝ "purity" favors the reading ΤΥΙỊΓ in the Eteocretan. The H is unfortunately incomplete. The text has  whereas a complete Π is . However, the horizontal stroke at the bottom of the letter fits the form of the H () but not of the Π in this text. The fragment on which the word is written has been lost but the horizontal line on the bottom of the letter is clear on the photograph. If the fragment is rediscovered, a cleaning should reveal more of the letter than is now legible on the photograph.

31. The only certain Eteocretan identification in the Second Dreros Bilingual so far is IHIA = γένοιτο. This establishes the Hebrew היה as the verb "to be" in the Dreros dialect and corroborates the Northwest Semitic character of the Dreros dialect with a crucial word. (The variant הוה is regular in Aramaic and rare in Hebrew. It is attested, though only once, in Ugaritic.) The Phoenician and Arabic verb "to be" is the root *kwn*, that occurs in specialized ways in Hebrew.

32. Having examined the bilingual evidence of the Semitic character of Eteocretan, we may now turn to the Eteocretan unilinguals from Praisos.[20] The earliest of them (ca. sixth century) is a boustrophedon inscription (beginning retrograde) of five lines (Plate III):

1) [ ]ΝΚΑΛ ΜΙΤ ΚẸ
2) ΟΣ . ΒΑΡΞΕ . Ạ[ ]Ο
3) [ ]ẠΡΚ[ ]ẠΓΣ ΕΤ . ΜΕ Υ Ṃ
4) ΑΡ ΚΡΚΟ ΚΛ ΕΣ̣ . Υ ΕΣ̣
5) [ ]ΑΣ ΕΓΥΝ ΑΝ(Α+Ι)Τ

33. In all three Praisos stones where the first line is preserved, we find MIT, the Semitic word for "died" (cf. Hebrew מת *mêt*). The inscriptions are accordingly funerary. The opening word is a personal name perhaps to be restored as [ΑΒΔ]ΝΚΑΛ corresponding to Ugaritic ᶜ*bdnkl* "Slave-of-the-(Moongoddess)-Nikkal." KẸ could stand for Hebrew *kī* "when"; ΟΣ, for Hebrew עז ᶜ*ōz* "strength, might" probably here in its special meaning of "pestilence" (see UT, text 54:13); ΒΑΡΞΕ is composed of *b*+'*arq*+*ze* = בארק ז "in this land." The opening words would thus mean "A. died when there was a pestilence in this land." In line 3, *ark* may well be '*arq* "land" (§76), the same word that occurs in the combination ΒΑΡΞΕ. Apparently]ΑΓΣ belongs to the verb, and ET would then be the particle introducing the object: ΜΕ Υ ṂΑΡ ΚΡΚΟ ΚΛ ΕΣ̣ . Υ ΕΣ̣[ ] "whoever he be,

[20] The Praisos texts have been published on pp. 138–141 of vol. III (1942) of M. Guarducci's *Inscriptiones Creticae*, La Libreria dello Stato, Rome, 1935–50 (to be continued).

fellow citizen; any man, and man - - -" (in Hebrew[21] [ ]מי הוא מר כרכו כל איש ואיש *mī hû mâr karkō kōl 'īš û-'īš*). The sense of this formula is clear because we have a variant in another Praisos text (§41).

34. The longest (or "Second") Eteocretan fragment is the following funerary stone from Praisos of about 300 B.C. (Plate IV):

1) ΟΝΑΔΕΣΙ ΕΜΕΤΕΠΙ ΜΙΤ ΣΦΑ
2) [Α] ΔΟΦ[ ]ΙΑΡΑΛΑ ΦΡΑΙΣΟΙΙΝΑΙ
3) [Ε]Φ̣ΕΣ ΤΝΜΤΟΡ ΣΑΡ ΔΟΦ ΣΑΝΟ
4) [ ]ΣΑΤΟ ΙΣΣΤ ΕΦΕΣ ΙΑΤ̣Ι̣ΥΝ
5) [ ]ΑΝΙΜΕΣΤΕΠΑΛΥΝ ΓΥ ΤΑΤ
6) ΣΑΝΟ ΜΟΣΕΛ ΟΣ ΦΡΑΙΣΟΝΑ̣
7) Τ̣ΣΑΑ ΔΟΦ ΤΕΝ[ ]Ο̣[ ]
8) [ ]ΜΑΠΡΑΙΝΑΙΡΕΡΕ̣[ ]
9) [ ]ΙΡΕΙΡΕΡΕΙΕΤ[ ]
10) [ ]ΝΤΙΡΑΝ Φ[ ]
11) [ ]ΑΣΚΕΣ[ ]
12) [ ]ΟΤ[ ]

35. The opening word, ΟΝΑΔΕΣ(Ι), is a personal name that appears in Cypriote Phoenician as אנתש *'ntš*.[22] The verb is again ΜΙΤ "died." The word ΔΟΦ appears thrice in the text, each time preceded by a Semitic numeral: ΣΦΑ[Α], ΣΑΡ, ΤΣΑΑ. ΣΦΑ[Α] = Hebrew שבע *š*^{e}*va*^{c} "7", ΣΑΡ = סר *sar*[23] "10", and ΤΣΑΑ = Hebrew תשע *t*^{e}*ša*^{c} "9." In lines 2 and 6, ΦΡΑΙΣΟ- refers to "Praisos", where the text was found.

36. While the context is not clear, ΜΤΟΡ in line 3 may prove to be the same as Eteocypriote *ma-to-ri* (§7).

37. ΣΑΝΟ (lines 3 and 6) is the 3 m. sg. demonstrative pronoun זנה "this" (= Eteocypriote *sa-na*; cf. §9). Note that "this" may be expressed pleonastically with ΣΑΝΟ before and ΟΣ after the noun: ΣΑΝΟ ΜΟΣΕΛ ΟΣ = זנה מושל אז "this ruler"; the same construction occurs in Eteocypriote *sa-na a-ri-si-to-no-se* (§§5, 17) "this Ariston".[24] ΜΟΣΕΛ = Hebrew מושל *mōšel* "ruler."

38. In line 4, ΕΦΕΣ ΙΑΤ̣Ι̣ΥΝ is to be compared with what would appear in Phoenician as אפס יאת(י)ון *'efes ya't(i)yûn* "they shall not come."

[21] Any person who knows Hebrew well, should understand what follows, though expressions like מר כרכו (instead of בן עירו) may sound quaint. Hebraists desiring orientation in Hebrew written in Latin and Greek letters, should study the valuable monograph by A. Sperber, "Hebrew Based upon Transliterations," *Hebrew Union College Annual* 12–13, 1937–38, pp. 103–274.

[22] See Z. S. Harris, *A Grammar of the Phoenician Language*, American Oriental Society, New Haven, 1936, p. 80.

[23] As in Aramaic תריסר "2+10" = "12." The root is עשר *^{c}śr*. It is conceivable that ΤΟΡΣΑΡ = תריסר "12" here.

[24] As noted above (§17, n.), this idiom is attested in Aramaic.

39. In the Third Praisos text (Plate V), the first 14 lines are preserved at the right but broken away at the left:

1)]Ξ̣ON Υ MIT
2)]ATAP KOMN
3)]PHΔHΣΔEΛ
4)]ΣΩΠEIPAPI
5)]Ẹ NTAΣATϜΣEΥ
6)]N NAΣ IPO KΛ EΣ
7)]IPEPMHIAMAPΦ
8)]ẸIPEPΦINΣΔAN
9)]MAMΔEΔI KAPK
10)]PIΣPAIPAPIΦ
11)]ỊṆNEI KAPΞ
12)]TAPIΔOHI
13)]ENBA
14)]ΔNAΣ
15) [ ]

40. Note again MIT "died" in the first line. The preceding Υ is the conjunction "and," written *u* in Punic that is spelled in Latin letters;[25] it is pronounced *û* in Hebrew (וּ). In the second line KOMN may be the same as KOMN in the First Dreros Bilingual (§23) where it seems to correspond to Greek *τυρός* "cheese" in which case KOMN is from Semitic *gbn* "cheese." KOMN occurs also in another Praisos text (§44).

41. The phrase in line 6 is synonymous with the variant we noted in §33: NAΣ IPO Υ KΛ EΣ = נש עירו וכל איש "the people of his city and every man" referring to all mankind, whether fellow citizens (of the deceased) or outsiders.

42. It is interesting to contrast KAPK = כרך "town" in line 9 with KAPΞ = כרך ז (*kark*+*z*) "this town" in line 11.

43. In line 12]TAPIΔOHI "drive him out"[26] probably refers to the expul-

[25] E.g., Plautus, Poenulus 930: *alonim u alonuth sicorathi* = *deos deasque veneror* (:950). Punic in Latin letters is not an isolated phenomenon limited to the Poenulus. The so-called Latino-Libyan inscriptions are also Punic written in Latin letters; see G. Levi Della Vida, "Sulle iscrizioni 'latino-libiche' della Tripolitania," *Oriens Antiquus* 2, 1963, pp. 65–94; and M. Sznycer, "Les inscriptions dites 'latino-libyques'," *Comptes Rendues du GLECS* 10, pp. 97–104, session of 16 June 1965. In those texts too, we find *u* "and." There are also Punic inscriptions written in Greek letters, such as the texts from Hofra near Constantine, Algeria; see C. H. Gordon, "The Mediterranean Factor (etc.)," pp. 22–23.

[26] The ending is *-û(hî)*, with *û* rather than *ô*, in the strong verb. The weak verbs *tertiae infirmae* have *ô* in Aramaic and Arabic. Perhaps analogy is at work. With the pl. noun, the ending is *-ôhî* in Aramaic (Daniel 5:1 et passim) and occasionally in Hebrew (Psalm 116:12). If we have a participle here ("his expellers"), there is no difficulty.

sion of anyone who dishonors the memory of the deceased. In line 14 ΔΝΑΣ looks like Aramaic דנש *d-nâš* "of people"; cf. also Arabic ناس *nâs-* "people."

44. In the next ("Fourth") Praisos fragment (Plate VI), note in line 7 the combination KOMN "cheese" which occurs in two other Eteocretan texts (§§23, 40):[27]

1)]APTIẠ[
2)]E[ ]AT[
3)]A[
4)]ΘEPT[
(blank)
5)]ḲOΣA[
6)]TEPN[
7)]KOMNE[
8)]ATATE[
9)]ΔEAPΣ[
(blank)

45. A unique digraphic Eteocretan text from Psychro[28] is to be dated around 300 B.C. (Plate VII). It is of singular importance because the scribe has rewritten the opening word (ΕΠΙΘΙ) in a late form of the Minoan syllabary (*i-pi-ti*) showing that on Crete, as well as on Cyprus, the remnant of the old population still remembered their native script, whose beginnings go back to around 1800 B.C.:

1) ΕΠΙΘΙ
2) Z ΗΘΑΝΘΗ
3) ΕΝΕΤΗ ΠΑΡΣΙΦΑΙ
4) *i-pi-ti*

46. Line one: ΕΠΙΘΙ = Phoenician הפתח *hptḥ* "the engraved monument." For E as the definite article that appears in Hebrew as *ha-*,[29] cf. Punic *esse*[30] (for

[27] Other possible readings are TAT (in line 8; cf. §34, line 5) = תחת *taḥat* "under" and ΑΡΣ (in line 9; cf. §48) = ארץ "earth."

[28] S. Marinatos, "Grammaton Didaskalia," in *Minoica* (= Sundwall Festschrift), Berlin, 1958, pp. 226–231 and pl. I; republished with facsimile by S. Davis, *The Phaistos Disk and the Eteocretan Inscriptions from Psychro and Praisos*, Witwatersrand University Press, Johannesburg, 1961, p. 26.

[29] We have already noted the interchange of *a* and *e* and their identity in the supralinear Babylonian Masorah. It remains to observe that Greek E is derived from ה *h* and occupies its position as the fifth letter in the alphabet.

[30] Poenulus 940, according to variant in the footnote, in the Oxford edition of *Plauti Comoediae II; macum esse* "this place" is rendered into Latin as *hanc urbem* (:950) providing the equation of Latin *hanc* = *esse*. The basic text has *macom syth* "this place" in which *syth* (זאת) is the fem. form of the demonstrative pronoun, as distinct from *esse* (הזה) which is masc. Neither variant can be accounted for as a scribal corruption; *macom syth* alongside *macum esse* must reflect a living tradition of writing Punic in Latin letters, for these variants are inner-Punic alternatives.

Hebrew הזה *hazze* "this"; literally "the this-one"). The laryngeal ח *ḥ* in פתח *ptḥ* "engraved monument" is lost consonantally, though it colors the vowel(s), in Eteocretan as in Akkadian and various Aramaic and Punic dialects.

47. Line two contains one of the most transparently Phoenician phrases in these texts. Z HΘANΘH = *z* + *yatantī* (which would be written ויתנת in Phoenician) "which + I have set".[31]

48. Line 3 is problematic and all that can now be done is to venture some suggestions in the hope that they may help others get closer to the truth. ENETE is possibly to be analyzed as E (<*ʿal* "over")[32] + NET (<*naḥt* "resting place") + H (= -*ī* "my"); i.e., "over my resting place." ΠΑΡΣΙΦΑΙ is also problematic but we may make a case for Π + ΑΡΣ + ΙΦΑΙ = *p* "in"[33] + *'arṣ* "land"[34] + *yfay* "beauty."[35]

49. The entire Psychro text, in accordance with the foregoing suggestions, would appear in Phoenician letters thus: הפתח ז יתנת ע(ל) נחתי בארץ יפי *hptḥ zytnt ʿ(l) nḥty b'rṣ ypy* "the engraved monument which I have set over my resting place in the Land of Beauty (= Elysian Fields)." While the interpretation of line 3 is uncertain, and lines 1 and 2 can be rendered either "I have set this engraved monument" or "the engraved monument which I have set," four key words are clear: E = ה "the," ΠΙΘΙ = Minoan *pi-te* = פתח "engraved monument," Z = Minoan *za* = ז "this" or "which," and *ytn* "to give, set" as in Minoan and Phoenician (יתן). All four words are found in Phoenician and three of them in Minoan as well.[36] Moreover this engraved stone preserves the ancient Minoan terminology attested on the Linear A engraved stones, which are called by the same noun that appears in Phoenician (פתח) and are described as given or placed by the same verb (יתן) that expresses this in comparable Phoenician texts. The Psychro text thus shows the continuity of the language and tradition since Minoan times. Psychro, where the Dictaean cave is located, is the site of a Minoan shrine where the cult was tenacious enough to perpetuate Minoanism into Hellenistic times.

50. Eteocretan consists of a group of closely related and mutually intelligible Northwest Semitic dialects. In orthography and dialect there are both local and

[31] Alternatively the Z could go with the preceding word so that the first two lines would equal Phoenician הפתח ז יתנת "this engraved monument I have given." For HΘANΘH (with *n*), note Ugaritic *ytnt* and Punic יתנתי.

[32] For the loss of the *l* in this preposition, see C. H. Gordon, *Archiv für Orientforschung* 12, 1938, p. 115, §69.

[33] The Semitic languages normally have *b*-; but cf. Mandaic *pat* for *bat* "daughter" (with *p*- for *b*-).

[34] See §44, line 9.

[35] The root is יפי *ypy*. The Phoenician evidence for many of the Eteocretan readings is presented in C. H. Gordon, "Eteocretan," *Journal of Near Eastern Studies* 21, 1962, pp. 211–214.

[36] See §§121, 124.

chronological differences.[37] Now that we have examined the sources, we shall outline the evidence for the orthography and grammar using only data that are certain or highly probable, and leaving aside the more provisional identifications.

[37] There are local differences of dialect and orthography at each Eteocretan site such as Dreros, Praisos and Psychro. We must also reckon with chronological developments; thus the early Praisos text (§32) is not identical with the later texts from the same site. Such matters will be brought out in Chapters V and VI.

IV. THE DEVELOPMENT AND TRANSMISSION OF THE ALPHABET ON CRETE

51. The archaic texts from Dreros (§§20–21, 28–29) and Praisos (§32) use Α, Ε, Ι, Ο and Υ — and only these five letters — as vowels. (Omega does not occur, and eta is strictly consonantal, until the later texts.) This five-vowel repertoire reflects precisely the same five vowels inherent in the Cretan syllabary. Thus when the Cretans adopted the consonantal Phoenician alphabet, they added to it the means of expressing the five vowels to which they had so long been accustomed from their long use of the native syllabary.

52. The development of the alphabet with vowels may have started with the Eteocretans who quite likely had closer relations than their Greek neighbors with the Phoenicians of Asia.[38] Yet the Cretan habit of writing Semitic (Linear A) and Greek (Linear B) in the same native syllabary had conditioned the two ethnic groups of the Cretan population to share the same script. The transmission of the alphabet from Semites to Greeks must have taken place in bilingual communities such as Dreros, and there must have been many such communities in central and especially eastern Crete.

53. The function of omicron is important in determining the origin of what we call the "Greek" alphabet. In shape and position within the alphabet, omicron corresponds to Phoenician ע *^{c}ayin*. In Crete since Middle Minoan times, *^{c}ayin* was pronounced *o* in words like *bôl* (<*ba^{c}l*) "Baal, lord"[39] and *nôl* (<*na^{c}l*) "sandal"[40] (§167). This was not the case in the standard dialects of Asia such as Phoenician, Hebrew, etc., where the ע remained consonantal. Accordingly, the evidence

[38] According to the terminology of the ancient Greeks, the Eteocretans were Phoenicians. When Herodotus (5:58) calls the alphabet used by the Greeks "Phoenician," he was not merely depending on already ancient traditions. In his time the Eteocretans were alive on Crete and in the course of inscribing texts like those we are now discussing. The Hellenistic Cretan historian Dosiadas should no longer be discredited because "nothing is known of the reasons on which he based his claim" that "the alphabet originated in Crete" (L. H. Jeffery, *The Local Scripts of Archaic Greece*, Clarendon Press, Oxford, 1961, p. 9). No reasons were needed in his time when the Eteocretan descendants of the Minoans were still living witnesses of what had taken place and of what was still common knowledge. In the fourth century A.D., Lucius Septimius recorded that in the thirteenth year of Nero, an earthquake at Knossos exposed the interior of the tomb ascribed to Dictys, bringing to light some inscriptions. The latter were delivered to Nero who regarded them as Phoenician and called in Semitists to interpret them (A. J. Evans, *Scripta Minoa* I, Clarendon Press, Oxford, 1909, p. 109). Accordingly the conclusions of the present monograph would have been regarded as obvious in Imperial Roman as well as in Hellenistic times.

[39] The divine name written *pu-rá* = "Bol" (§163) as in Palmyrene (e.g., "Yarḥî-Bôl").

[40] "Glove" is also conceivable in the Phaistos Disc.

points to Crete as the place where *ʿayin/omicron* had the value *o*. This adds to the mounting evidence that Crete was where the Phoenician consonantal alphabet was equipped with vowels and developed into what we call the Greek alphabet.

54. It remains to comment on Υ. The accepted view has it that only from alpha through tau are the Greek letters borrowed from Phoenician, because they follow the order of the letters in the familiar Phoenician/Hebrew alphabet that ends with *t*. However, it is striking that the same alphabet with the same order of the letters is attested in the longer Ugaritic ABC of the 14th century B.C.[41] In the Ugaritic alphabet, *u* comes after *t*. It is quite likely that the "Greek" alphabet is based on an earlier and longer Semitic ABC than the conventional Hebrew ABC of twenty-two letters ending in *t*. This is all the more likely because Υ (but not Φ, X, Ψ, Ω) is used in the earliest epichoric inscriptions such as the Dreros bilinguals (§§20–21, 28–29) and the early Praisos text (§32). We may therefore have to speak of the Greek letters from A to Υ (and not merely from A to T) as being borrowed in their present order from a Semitic alphabet.

[41] UT, p. 11, §3.1. The Ugaritic alphabet is consistently recorded on a number of tablets as follows: *a b g ḫ d h w z ḥ ṭ y k š l m ḏ n ẓ s ᶜ p ṣ q r ṯ ǵ t i u ś*. For the relation between this alphabet and the ABC of the Phoenicians and Hebrews, see UT, p. 12, §3.2. For the relation with the Greek and Latin ABCs, see *Scientific American*, Feb. 1965, p. 110.

V. ETEOCRETAN ORTHOGRAPHY

55. The labial stops are not distinguished clearly. Only in the earliest texts does Β appear (§§20, 28). Later Π and Φ correspond to *b* (*v*) as well as *p* (*f*). Φ, which occurs only in the later texts, covers *v* as well as *f*: ΣΦΑ[Α] = Hebrew שבע *š*ᵉ*va*ᶜ "7" and ΕΦΕΣ = Hebrew אפס *'efes*. For Π = *b*, see §48.

56. For the dental stops, it is necessary to note only that the emphatic *ṭ* is not distinguished from the nonemphatic surd *t*:]ΤΑΡΙΔΟΗΙ and (if the Η is correct) ΤΥΗ̣Ρ are derived from טרד *ṭrd* "to drive out" and טהר *ṭhr* "pure," respectively. Examples of Τ = *t*: ΕΤ = Hebrew את *'et* (§23), ΤΣΑΑ = Hebrew תשע *t*ᵉ*ša*ᶜ "9" (§35).

57. Except in the Psychro text, all the sibilants are covered by Σ: (1) *s*: ΕΦΕΣ = Hebrew אפס *'efes*; (2) *z*: ΟΣ = Phoenician אז *'oz* (§37); (3) *š*: ΣΦΑ[Α] = Hebrew שׁבע *š*ᵉ*va*ᶜ "7" (§35); (4) *ś*: ΣΑΡ = סר *sr* "10" (§35; derived from עשר *ᶜśr*); (5) *ṣ*: ΑΡΣ (§48; derived from ארץ *'rṣ*); see also §44. In the Psychro text, Hebrew/Phoenician ז *z* is written Ζ (§47).

58. As in the case of the dentals, so too of the palatals, the emphatic (*q*) is not distinguished from the nonemphatic surd (*k*): ΑΡΚ = ארק *'arq* (§33) "land" with emphatic *q*, while ΚΑΡΚ (§§33, 42) = כרך *kark* "town" with surd *k*.

59. In the earlier texts, eta is not a vowel but the laryngeal consonant *h*: ΜΗΡ may correspond to Hebrew מהר *mahēr*; ΙΗΙΑ definitely corresponds to Hebrew יהיה *yihye* (§30), and -ΤΑΡΙΔΟΗΙ (§43) to Aramaic טרדוהי *-ṭarridôhī*.

60. At the end of a syllable, ע (ᶜayin) is represented by Α in ΤΣΑΑ = Hebrew תשע *t*ᵉ*ša*ᶜ (§35) and ΡΙΑ = Hebrew רע *rē*ᵃᶜ (§24). Similarly א (*'alef*) may be represented by Α when closing the syllable: ΙΑΤ̣Ι̣ΥΝ = Hebrew יאתיון *y'tywn* (§38) but t is also possible to interpret the Α as the original vowel with the prefix *ya-*, preserved by the following 'alef.

61. At the beginning of a syllable, none of the laryngeals are represented orthographically: (1) the ' is not indicated in ΕΤ = Hebrew את *'et* (§23), ΕΣ = Hebrew אש (as in אֶשְׁבַּעַל "Man-of-Baal") (§§33, 41), ΙΣΑ = Hebrew אשה *'iššā* "woman" (§24), ΕΦΕΣ = Hebrew אפס *'efes* (§38); (2) the ᶜ is not indicated in ΙΡ = Hebrew עיר *ᶜîr* "city" (§41); (3) nor the *h* in Ε (from *ha* "the"; §46); (4) nor the *ḥ* in ΑΒΡ = Hebrew חבר *ḥābēr* "companion" (§24).

62. The semivowels *y* and *w* are represented as Ι and Ϝ respectively. Thus ΙΑΤ̣Ι̣ΥΝ = *ya't(i)yûn* (§38) and ΙΗΙΑ, pronounced *'ihya* (§30). The digamma occurs in texts from Dreros (§20) and Praisos (§39).

63. Short *a* is expressed by Α: ΤΣΑΑ = Hebrew תשע *t*ᵉ*ša*ᶜ (§35), ΣΦΑ[Α] = Hebrew שבע *š*ᵉ*va*ᶜ (§35), ΑΒΡ = Hebrew חבר *ḥābēr* (§24) < *ḥabir*, etc. Final *-ā* ("anceps") also appears as Α: ΙΣΑ = Hebrew אשה *'iššā* "woman" (§24). Long *â* is indicated by Α in ΝΑΣ, pronounced *nâš* "people" (§§41, 43).

64. Iota indicates short or long *i*; (1) short *i*: ΙΣΑ = Hebrew אשה *'iššā* (§24), IHIA, pronounced *'ihya* (§30); (2) long *î*: IP = Hebrew עיר *ʿîr* (§41). Iota also corresponds to long ṣere (*ê*) in Hebrew regardless of whether it is reduced from the diphthong *ay*; in PIA = Hebrew רע *rêaʿ* (§24) and MIT = Hebrew מֵת *mêt* (§§33, 35, 40), the vowel is long because it remains in distant, open syllables;[42] in INAI = Hebrew עיני *ʿênê* (§26), the first I corresponds to Hebrew *ê* reduced from *ay* (as in Arabic عَيْن *ʿayn-* "eye").

65. In the Psychro text (§45), H stands for *î* in ΗΘΑΝΘΗ = *îtʰantʰî* "which I have set," and perhaps in ENETH = *ʿenne(ḥ)tî* (<*ʿal naḥtî*) "over my resting place." In the older Praisos text (§32), E possibly stands for long *î* in ME = Hebrew מי *mî* "who(ever)," and in KE = Hebrew כי *kî* "when, because."

66. Northwest Semitic *e* is represented by epsilon: ET = Hebrew את *'et* (§23), ΕΦΕΣ = Hebrew אפס *'efes* (§38), MEN = Syriac ܡܶܢ *men* (§26), the final syllable of ΒΑΡΞΕ (§33) = Hebrew זה *ze* "this," ΕΣ = Hebrew אש *'eš* "man" (§33) as in the personal name אֶשְׁבַּעַל "Eshbaal" (meaning "Man-of-Baal"; e.g., 1 Chronicles 8:33).

67. The *u* comes in as Υ; short *u*: in the problematic (§30) ΤΥΗ̣Ρ = Semitic *ṭuhr* "purity"; long *û*: Υ = Hebrew ו *û* "and" (§33), ΙΑΤ̣ΙΥΝ = יאתיון *ya't(i)yûn* "they will come."

68. Omicron occurs for *o*, whether it be developed from *u* (as perhaps in ΟΣ = Hebrew עז *ʿōz* from **ʿuzz*); or from *a* (as in ΟΣ = אז *'oz* from **'az*) because of the accent; see §§10, 17. In the following examples, O stands for long *ô* reduced from the diphthong *aw*: ΛΑΜΟ = Hebrew *lʾimmō* (-*ō*<-*ahu* with elision of the *h*), -ΤΑΡΙΔΟΗΙ = טרדוהי -*ṭarridôhî* (-*ôhî*<-*awhû*); see §§22, 43, 59.

69. The diphthong *ay* may possibly be preserved at the end of a Semitic word in INAI = Semitic *ʿaynay* "eyes (of)" (§26), and ΙΦΑΙ from יפי *yafay* "beauty, beautiful" (§48). It occurs also in the name ΦΡΑΙΣΟ "Praisos." The diphthong *aw* is preserved only at the end of the following word:]ΙΡΜΑϜ (§20). Otherwise it is reduced to *ô* (§85).

70. The only letter for expressing *o*, long or short, is omicron in the older texts. The sole occurrence of omega so far is in a later text from Praisos (§39).

71. A number of spirants can be used vocalically in Eteocretan (§73), so that M, N, Λ, P and Σ are sometimes to be normalized as vowels (*m̥*, *n̥*, *l̥*, *r̥*, *s̥*).

72. Neither consonantal nor vocalic length is indicated orthographically. Thus ΛΑΜΟ = *lm̥mō* "for his mother" (§22), -ΤΑΡΙΔ- = -*ṭarrid*- (§43), ΝΑΣ = *nâš* "people" (§41), IP = *ʿîr* "city" (§41). Since Eteocretan texts do not double consonants in the orthography, it is apparent that orthographic gemination to indicate phonetically doubled consonants is a Greek innovation.

[42] Semitists will find the evidence in Judges 11:37, 38; Psalm 45:15; and in Isaiah 22:2; Psalm 143:3; Lamentations 3:6. Short vowels are reduced to zero (*šwa*) in distant, open syllables (i.e., open syllables that are neither accented nor just before the accent).

VI. ETEOCRETAN PHONETICS

73. The most striking feature of Eteocretan phonetics is the vocalic use of a number of sounds that are generally regarded as strictly consonantal. Note the vocalic function of *m*, *n*, *l*, *r* and *s* in the following words: MHP = *m̥hr̥* "quickly", KOMN = *komn̥* "cheese", ΛMO = *lm̥mō* "for his mother," KΛ = *kl̥* "all," KPK = *kr̥k* "town" (§§33, 42); the second *s* in IΣΣT (§34) is apparently *s̥*, whatever the meaning. It is precisely these consonants (*m*, *n*, *l*, *r*, *s*) that are omitted at the end of syllables in Linear B and the phenomenon is to be explained on the grounds of the Minoan substratum. For example, the reason that the Linear B *ka*-sign has the value *kal* in *ka-ko* (= χαλκός) is that the *ka*-sign depicts a "wheel" (גלגל *galgal* in Hebrew), which in Minoan was pronounced *gl̥gl̥*. Accordingly the WHEEL-sign originally had the value *gl̥* or *kl̥*. Not all signs may have represented words with a vocalic consonant; but analogy could take care of the rest: i.e., *ka* : *kl̥* : : *pa* : *X* (whereby, *X* = *pl̥*, even though the *pa*-sign designates a word that begins with *pa* and has no *l* in it).

74. The labials confront us with some shifts. In the early texts from Dreros (§§20–31) B occurs for Semitic *b* in ABP = Hebrew חבר *ḥābēr* "companion." Also the preposition ב *b* "in" appears as B (§33) in the early Praisos text. But in the late text from Psychro where ΠAPΣ may possibly stand for בארץ *b'arṣ* "in (the) land (of)," it has apparently shifted to *p* (§48). It is striking that B occurs in none of the later texts. It thus seems that between 600 and 300 B.C., B lost its voicing. Thereafter not only does Π stand for etymological *p* or *b*, but so does Φ; for EΦEΣ is derived from *'ps*, whereas ΣΦA[A] is derived from *šbᶜ* (§§35, 38).

75. The nature of Φ requires discussion. Was it pronounced p^h (that is, aspirated *p* as in English) or *f*? The Psychro (§45) and later Praisos (§§34, 39) texts favor the pronunciation *f* because Φ is distinguished from Π, which occurs frequently in the same texts. However, the problem is complicated by the Psychro text, in which *îtantī* is written HΘANΘH, with both *t*'s written Θ. That the first *t* was spirantized to *ṯ* is quite possible; but not so the second *t*, which follows consonantal *n*. The rule for spirantizing *t* (as well as *d*, *b*, *p*, *k*, *g*) is that the process takes place when the consonant is short (i.e., not doubled) and follows a vowel. Accordingly, the Θ for the second *t* indicates, it would seem, aspiration (i.e., t^h) rather than spirantization (*ṯ*). Regardless of how we are to interpret the process, it does not take place with a *t* that was originally preceded by *ḥ*, if our provisional explanation of ENETH in the Psychro text is right; thus note T (not Θ) in NETH (<*naḥtī*); §48.

76. Etymological ض *ḍ* appears in the early Praisos text as K (§33) which

must be ק *q* as in Old Aramaic, Yaudian and (for the particular word in question) Mandaic. ΒΑΡΞΕ contains ארק *'arq* "land." Later we seem to find ΑΡΣ = ארץ *'arṣ* in the Psychro text (§48), and perhaps in the Fourth Praisos fragment (§44), with the shift of the original *ḏ* to *ṣ* as in Phoenician, Ugaritic, Hebrew, etc.

77. The failure of the *n* to assimilate to the second *t* in ΗΘΑΝΘΗ (§47) occurs in Punic; and regularly in Ugaritic for this particular word (*ytn* "to give, set").

78. K stands for etymological *g* in ΚΟΜΝ (from *gbn*) "cheese" (§§23, 40, 44). It looks very much as if the voiced stops shifted to surds in Eteocretan. Gamma, to be sure, does occur (though rarely); but it seems to be a positional variant with nothing to do with etymology; thus ΕΓΥΝ (< **yakûn*) with original *k* becoming voiced *g* intervocalically (§32).

79. To what extent the laryngeals survived in Eteocretan must be deduced from the orthographic facts (§§59–61). It appears that *ḥ* did not survive as such at the beginning or end of the syllable: ΑΒΡ = Hebrew חבר *ḥābēr*, perhaps ΝΕΤΗ = Phoenician נחתי *naḥtī* "my resting place," and certainly ΠΙΘΙ = Phoenician פתח *ptḥ* "engraved monument" (§§24, 46–50).

80. The laryngeals are to a great extent concealed by the orthography. Thus the vowel letters in Eteocretan continue Minoan usage (§61) in standing for open syllables beginning with a glottal catch ('alef) or laryngeal such as *h*. Greek continues this tradition, for though the use of uncials conceals the "laryngeals," normal Greek usage adds smooth or rough breathing, showing that the Greeks felt an initial vowel sign was not simply a vowel but a syllable beginning with ' or *h*.

81. The aphaeresis of initial ᶜ(*a*) in the numeral ΣΑΡ (from עשר *ᶜ*aśar*) occurs in sandhi in Aramaic תריסר *trê-sar* "12" (§35).

82. Initial *yi-* shifts to *'i-* in Eteocretan ΙΗΙΑ (= Hebrew יהיה *yihye* "it will be") which is translated *γένοιτο* "let there be" (§31). This occurs regularly in Akkadian (where **yašma*ᶜ becomes *išmê* "he hears, heard") and sporadically throughout Northwest Semitic, starting with Minoan (§148). The Septuagint pronunciation of Hebrew observes this shift and has thereby left its stamp on biblical names such as Hebrew יצחק *Yiṣḥāq* = ΙΣΑΑΚ "Isaac." This is not the case with names in *Ya-*: יעקב *Ya*ᶜᵃ*qōb* = ΙΑΚΩΒ "Jacob", even as **ya't*(*i*)*yûn* comes into Eteocretan as ΙΑṬΙ̣ΥΝ (§38).

83. Hebrew *ê* (which is never reduced to šwa, or zero vowel, in distant open syllables) is treated like *î* (§64).

84. The uncontracted diphthong *aw* appears in the verbal form]Ι̣ΡΜΑϜ (§25).

85. The 3 m. sg. possessive suffix is *-ō* (§22) as in Hebrew, going back to *-ahu* (>*-au*>*-ō*). This also takes place in Eteocypriote *a-lo* (§14) "over him" which goes back to *ᶜ*alayhu*. The Hebrew consonantal orthography (עליו) preserves the *-y-* though the standard Masoretic pronunciation calls for reading

ᶜ*ālāw* (עָלָיו). Eteocypriote thus goes farther than Hebrew by further reducing this *aw* to *ō*.

86. With the exception of the place name ΦΡΑΙΣΟ (§35) "Praisos," diphthongs have so far been attested only at the ends of words. We have noted]ỊΡΜΑϜ above (§84). The diphthong *ay* is preserved finally in ΙΝΑΙ and ΙΦΑΙ (§69). Otherwise *aw* shifts to *ō* (in addition to ΛΜΟ, note]ΤΑΡΙΔΟΗΙ in which the *ô* goes back to **aw*) and *ay* to Ι as in ΙΝΑΙ (< *ᶜ*aynay*); see §§67, 85.

87. The only anaptyctic vowel is the second Ε in ΕΦΕΣ (§38). This anaptyxis does not take place in other monosyllabic words such as segolate nouns: ΑΡΣ "land" (vs. Hebrew ארץ *'ereṣ*), similarly ΚΑΡΚ "town"; the same holds for ΤΥḤΡ (vs. Hebrew טהר *ṭōhar*); see §§30, 42, 48.

VII. ETEOCRETAN MORPHOLOGY

88. The independent personal pronoun "he" is written Υ (pronounced *hū*): ME Υ = מי הוא *mī hū* "whoever he be" (§33).

89. Suffixed 3 m. sg. personal pronoun *-ō* "his": KAPKO = כרכו (§33) or IPO = עירו "his city" (§41) and ΛΜΟ = לאמו "for his mother" (§22). Original *-hū* is dissimilated to *-hī* because of the preceding **-aw->-ô-* in]TAPIΔOHI = טרדוהי["expel him" (§43).

90. The independent pronoun "this" is ΣΑΝΟ = זנה (§37) (cf. Eteocypriote *sa-na* in §9) in the m. sg. (cf. Old Aramaic זנה *znh*, Phoenician זן *zn*); enclitic "this" is ΟΣ (Cypriote Phoenician אז). The f. sg. of the independent form appears as Eteocypriote *so-ti* "this" (= Hebrew זאת *zôt*; §13). In the older text from Praisos (§32) we find enclitic *ze* "this": BAPΞE "in this land"; it is shortened to *z*/*s* in the later texts: KAPΞ "this town" (§42; the enclitic is written ז *z* in standard Phoenician but dialectally ס *s* also appears).

91. The definite article occurs in EΠΙΘΙ (§46) "the engraved monument" (E = Hebrew ה *ha-*).

92. The proclitic relative pronoun Z (Phoenician ז *z*) may be attested in ΖΗΘΑΝΘΗ "which I have set" (§47) but it is also possible to take this as demonstrative ז ("I have given this engraved monument").

93. The interrogative pronoun *mī* "who?" is used indefinitely in ME Υ = מי הוא "whoever he be" (§33).

94. "All, every" is expressed by ΚΛ (Semitic *kull-*) followed by a noun in ΚΛ ΕΣ "every man" (pronounced *kḷ 'eš* but corresponding idiomatically to Hebrew כל איש *kol 'îš*; §§33, 41).

95. Three numerals are attested: "7": ΣΦΑ[Α] (Hebrew שבע *šb*ᶜ); "9": ΤΣΑΑ (Hebrew תשע *tš*ᶜ); "10": ΣΑΡ (Aramaic סר as in תריסר *trê-sar* "12," from ᶜ*śr*); see §§35, 55, 60, 81.

96. The loss of the original short, unaccented final vowels has stripped the noun of its case endings. Thus a form like KAPK can stand for original *karku* (nom.), *karki* (gen.), *karka* (acc.).

97. The f. sg. ending in the absolute state is *-ā* as in Hebrew: ΙΣΑ = Hebrew אשה *'iššā* "woman" (§24). (Eteocypriote *ka-i-li-po-ti* "as a memorial monument" is a more conservative form with the original *-t* preserved by the gen. case ending *-i*; §15.)

98. The biconsonantal noun ΕΣ is not the same in form as its common Hebrew cognate איש *'îš* "man" but tallies rather with the shorter form אש *'eš* as in the personal name "Eshbaal" (§66). (איש and אש have nothing to do in origin with אשה *'iššā* "woman"; the latter is derived from the root *'nṯ* as in أُنْثَى "female.")

99. Monosyllabic words are not "segolated" (§87) with the exception of ΕΦΕΣ.[43]

100. Biconsonantal nouns with medial long vowel: ΝΑΣ (=Aramaic נש *nâš*,[44] cf. Arabic ناس *nâs*) "people" (§§41, 72), ΙΡ (=Hebrew עיר *ᶜîr*) "city" (§41), ΡΙΑ (=Hebrew רע *rêaᶜ*) "friend" (§24). It is natural to take ΜΑΡ in the sense of Aramaic מר *mâr* "lord." The formula in which it occurs is ΜΕ Υ ΜΑΡ ΚΡΚΟ ΚΛ ΕΣ Υ ΕΣ (§33) and may be translated literally "lord of his town, every man and man [ ]." The expression is a merism (a set of antonyms implying totality) meaning "everybody." The question arises whether it should be paraphrased "king and commoner" or "fellow citizen and outsider." That the latter is correct is indicated by the variant ΝΑΣ ΙΡΟ Υ ΚΛ ΕΣ "the people of his city and any man" (§41). Citizens can be called "lords of the city" in Northwest Semitic.[45]

101. A biconsonantal noun, **ḥabir*>Hebrew חבר *ḥābēr*, appears in Eteocretan as ΑΒΡ (§24) "companion."

102. The gentilic suffix **-îy* may be present in ΦΡΑΙΣΟΙ (§34) where ΦΡΑΙΣΟ is "Praisos," and I makes the word mean "Praisonian."

103. The perfect tense of a transitive verb is used in ΗΘΑΝΘΗ "I have given" (§47)=*îtantī* from **yatantī* (written יתנתי *ytnty* in Punic).

104. With the intransitive verb, the perfect and participle have the same form in the 3 m. sg.: ΜΙΤ (§33) "(he) died".

105. The imperfect is attested in ΙΗΙΑ "he will be" (§30), and ΙΑΤ̣Ι̣ΥΝ (§38) "they will come". Perhaps]ΤΑΡΙΔΟΗΙ (§43) is to be read [*î*]*ṭarridôhī* (for **yaṭarridûhī*< **yaṭarridûhū*) "they shall expel him." Whether ΕΓΥΝ is to be equated with **yakûn* (Phoenician יכן *ykn*) "he will be" (§32) is uncertain; if so, then Eteocretan uses both verbs (היה *hāyā* as in Hebrew, and כן *kân* as in Phoenician and Arabic) for "to be."

106. The preposition ל *l-* "to, for" appears as ΛΥ before consonants (ΛΥΡΙΑ "to a friend" and as Λ before vowels (ΛΑΒΡ "to a companion"; §24).

107. The preposition *b-* "in" appears as Β (later Π) before vowels (§§33, 48).

108. The preposition مِن *men* "from" is written ΜΕΝ (§26).

109. Possibly the adverb that appears in Hebrew as מהר *mahēr* "quickly" is written ΜΗΡ, giving the verb ΙΗΙΑ the nuance of the optative *γένοιτο* (§30).

110. The coordinating conjunction is Υ "and" (=Punic ΟΥ *u*;[46] Hebrew ו *ū*); see §§33, 41.

111. The causal/temporal conjunction ΚΕ̣ (=Hebrew *kī*) occurs in ΚΕ̣ ΟΖ ΒΑΡΞΕ "when there was a pestilence in this land" (§33), if the reading is right.

[43] The word is originally a noun meaning "end" (as in Hebrew and Ugaritic).

[44] As in בר נש "son of man=human being."

[45] For "citizens" called "lords" of the city, note בעלי שכם (Judges 9:2, 3, 6, 7) "the citizens of Shechem."

[46] ΟΥ occurs in the Hofra texts, while *u* occurs in Poenulus and Latino-Libyan.

112. The sign of the definite accusative is prepositive ET (=Hebrew את *'et*): ET KOMN = *τὸν τυρόν* (§23).

113. The number, quality and variety of established readings in Eteocretan leave no doubt as to its Northwest Semitic character. In the following list of selected words, contextual evidence is strong and in five key instances is corroborated bilingually:

ABP	=	חבר	"companion"
E	=	ה	"the"
EΣ	=	אש	"man"
ET	=	את	(sign of acc.)
Z	=	ז	"this"
HΘANΘH	=	יתנתי	"I have given"
IHIA	=	יהיה	"it will be"
IP	=	עיר	"city"
KAPK	=	כרך	"town"
KΛ	=	כל	"all"
KOMN	=	جُبْن، גבינה	"cheese"
Λ	=	ל	"to, for"
-M-	=	אם	"mother"
MIT	=	מת	"died"
MOΣEΛ	=	מושל	"ruler"
NAΣ	=	נש	"people"
-O	=	-וֹ	"his"
OΣ	=	אז	"this"
ΠIΘI	=	פתח	"engraved monument"
PIA	=	רע	"friend"
ΣANO	=	זנה	"this"
ΣAP	=	סר	"10"
ΣΦA[A]	=	שבע	"7"
TΣAA	=	תשע	"9"
Υ-	=	-ו	"and"

VIII. THE DECIPHERMENT OF MINOAN

114. The decipherment of Mycenaean Linear B by Michael Ventris in 1952 was confirmed by a "virtual bilingual" from Pylos in which various pots are drawn pictographically as well as defined syllabically in Mycenaean Greek.[47] The detailed correctness of the Greek readings leave no doubt that Ventris's values for the signs are essentially right. Since most of the Linear A signs recur in Linear B with the same phonetic values,[48] Ventris's decipherment enables us to pronounce many names and words in the Minoan Linear A texts. The problem of deciphering Minoan thus resolves itself into fixing by context the meanings of pronounceable Minoan words and phrases to establish the identity of the language, which can be done if Minoan belongs to a known linguistic family.

115. Fortunately we have virtual bilinguals in Linear A. Like the Pylos tablet that confirmed the decipherment of Linear B, there is a Linear A tablet (Plate VII) from HT (Hagia Triada) with pictographs of pots accompanied by their Minoan names spelled syllabically. Out of the five legible pot names on that tablet (HT 31) four are Semitic: *qa-pà* = Hebrew כף[49] *kp* or Akkadian *kappu*, *su-pu* = Hebrew and Ugaritic סף *sp*, *ka-ro-pà* = Akkadian *karpu*[50] (cf. Ugaritic *krpn*), and *su-pà-ra* = Hebrew and Ugaritic ספל *spl*.

116. There is another virtual bilingual of a different sort (Plate VIII). The WHEAT determinative following *ku-ni-su* tells us that the word means "wheat."[51] In Akkadian *ku*(*n*)*nišu* means "emmer wheat." Its Aramaic cognate כונתא (a masculine noun from the Semitic root **knt*) is defined as "spelt" wheat. Now *si-to* followed by the same WHEAT determinative in Linear B = σῖτος. This shows that Minoan *ku-ni-su* = Mycenaean *si-to*; both can designate "wheat" in Semitic and Greek, respectively. Via the WHEAT determinative we accordingly have a Greco-Semitic equation.

[47] See Ventris and Chadwick, *Documents in Mycenaean Greek*, p. 336.

[48] This is proved by the same proper names that appear in both Linear A and B. E.g., *pa-i-to* "Phaistos" occurs in both A and B, implying that each sign has the same sound in the Minoan as in the Mycenaean texts. For further evidence, see E. Peruzzi, "Le Iscrizioni Minoiche," reprinted from *Atti dell'Accademia Toscana di Scienze e Lettere "La Columbaria"* 24, 1959–60, p. 34.

[49] For designating a kind of vessel, see Exodus 25:29; 37:16; Numbers 4:7; 7:14; etc. The pictograph is the general one for "vessel" appearing thrice on HT 31 for various vessels. The sign transliterated *qa* is not meant to imply ק; we are simply following the transliteration currently used for Linear B.

[50] The second vowel of *ka-ro-pà* is dropped in Akkadian *karpu* like all short unaccented vowels between single consonants in Akkadian.

[51] References to the Minoan words and names cited in this monograph are listed §163.

117. Other Minoan words can be defined from context. Thus totals are labeled *ku-ro* = Semitic *kull-* (e.g., Hebrew כל *kl*) "all." Text HT 88 gives the following sum (Plate VIII):

ki-ro .	*ku-pà-nu*	*1*
	ka-x	*1*
	ku-pà-nu	*1*
	pa-ya-re	*1*
	sa-ma-ro	*1*
	da-ta-re	*1*
ku-ro		*6*

with *ku-ro* designating the "total." Cf. the use of כל in Joshua 12:24 and especially הכל "the total" in Ezra 2:42.

118. HT 122 has a total of 31 (*ku-ro 31*) on the obverse, and another total of 65 (*ku-ro 65*) on the reverse. The two totals are combined to form *po-to-ku-ro 96* "grandtotal: 96" (Plate VIII). The meaning "grandtotal" is fixed by context but it remains to explain the first element *po-to*. We know that the word for "son" was pronounced *bun-* in Ugaritic.[52] The feminine *_bunt-_ would become *butt-* (with *nt*>*tt*). Tentatively we suggest that *po-to-ku-ro* stands for what would appear in Hebrew script as בת כל "daughter of all" = "grandtotal." "Son" and "daughter" are often used as the first element of compound nouns in Semitic.

119. A little magic bowl (Plate IX) from Knossos (text II,2)[53] opens with the word *a-ka-nu* = Hebrew and Aramaic אגן *'aggân* "bowl," which happens to be applied specifically to a magic bowl in an Aramaic incantation.[54] Magic bowls sometimes start with a formula indicating that the bowl is designed to repel evil from the client.[55] We are apparently dealing with such a formula here (see §156).

120. There are eighteen inscribed stone cult objects from various Minoan sites in eastern and central Crete. They are important because they are in one and the same language as is clear from recurrent formulae in them.[56] It is quite possible

[52] See UT §19.481. Note also Cypriote *pu-nu-to-so* = בן חדש and *βυν* = בן "son" in the Punic texts from Hofra (§18, n. 10; §40, n. 25).

[53] Inscribing incantations in ink inside clay bowls, though widespread, is especially well-attested in pre-Islamic Babylonia. The praxis is similar in Crete and Babylonia; e.g., the Knossos magic bowls (II,1; II,2) were found inverted and under the floor as in Babylonia. The standard work on the Babylonian bowls is J. A. Montgomery, *Aramaic Incantation Texts from Nippur*, University Museum, Philadelphia, 1913.

[54] Note *ag-gan-nu* in lines 5 and 9 of the Uruk incantation (*Orientalia* 9, 1940, p. 36).

[55] Thus texts 9, 14 and 30 in W. H. Rossell, *A Handbook of Aramaic Magical Texts*, Shelton College, Ringwood, N. J., 1953.

[56] See the table of recurrent phrases in Brice, *op. cit.*, pl. XXa.

that the so-called Linear A texts are in more than one language,[57] even as the Ugaritic script is used not only for writing the Ugaritic language but also Hurrian and Akkadian. Accordingly we may define Minoan as the official language of all Minoan Crete, used at all the shrines where Linear A dedications have been found on cult objects so far.

121. Several stone cult objects are inscribed with dedications that begin with *ya-ta-no-* (var. *a-ta-no-*[58]) = Phoenician יתן *yatan-* "he has given/donated." A libation bowl (I,14; see Plate IX) begins with *ya-ta-no-x u ya-*[ ]: a formula that recalls Phoenician יתן ויטנא *ytn wyṭn'* "he has given and set up as a votive offering."[59] Note that the conjunction "and" appears as *u*, as in Punic and Akkadian and sometimes in Ugaritic, Hebrew and Aramaic.[60]

122. A libation table from Knossos (I,8; Plate IX) contains the formula *ta-nu-a-ti ya-sa-sa-ra-ma-na*, which I am inclined to translate "I have set up this votive offering." The verb טנא *ṭn'* "to set up (as a votive offering)" is common in Phoenician dedications.[61] *Ya-sa-sa-ra-ma-na* contains the word *yašašalam-* (which occurs on seven of the eighteen cult objects). Most scholars have taken it to be the name of a deity. However, another possibility deserves consideration. It could be the noun for "votive offering"; the Š causative of the root *šlm* means "to make a delivery" in Ugaritic; there are nouns with the prefix *y-*.[62] Accordingly, *yašašalam-* might mean "what is delivered (to a god)" = "votive offering." The ending *-ânā* (in *yašašalamânā*) seems to correspond to Syriac *hânā* "this" which can follow the noun.[63]

123. Pithoi for wine have been found at Knossos; see texts II,6 ii & iii, for the WINE determinative inscribed on them.[64] One of the pithoi bears an inscription that includes the two syllable word *ya-ne*, flanked by a word divider on each side (Plate X). This is the way *yayn-* (Hebrew יין) "wine" would be spelled according to the orthographic rules deduced for Linear B.[65] Therefore the mean-

[57] Hurrian, Egyptian and Akkadian are historically conceivable as well as Indo-European dialects.

[58] The final syllable ("*x*") of (*y*)*a-ta-no-x* may represent the pronominal object (normally m. *-hu*, or f. *-ha*; but in Phoenician dialects also m. *-yu*, f. *-ya*) so that the whole word means "he gave it (i.e., the votive offering)." For *'atan-* as a variant of *yatan-*, see §148. Since no one Cretan site confronts us with both *yatan-* and *'atan-*, the difference may be local. However, the texts are too limited to provide a statistical basis for dividing Minoan into local dialects.

[59] See texts 33:2; 39:2; 41:1–2 in the edition of Donner and Röllig.

[60] Cf. UT §19.3.

[61] Donner and Röllig, *op. cit.*, III, p. 9, list 47 occurrences.

[62] E.g., Hebrew ילקוט *yalqûṭ* "bag," Arabic يربوع *yarbû*ᶜ "jerboa"; and numerous names such as "Isaac," "Jacob" and "Israel."

[63] "This king" can be expressed as ܗܢܐ ܡܠܟܐ *hânā malkā* or ܡܠܟܐ ܗܢܐ *malkā hânā.*

[64] Another has been excavated by John Caskey on the island of Kea (Keos).

[65] Ventris and Chadwick, *op. cit.*, p. 43.

ing of *ya-ne* as "wine" is not only possible orthographically but it is favored by its presence on a wine pithos found at a site where similar pithoi bear the WINE determinative.

124. One reading is especially significant because it shows the linguistic continuity from Minoan to Eteocretan.[66] An inscribed libation table from Palaikastro (I,4:b) refers to itself as . *pi-te za* . (with a word divider on each side) = Phoenician פתח ז "this engraved monument."[67] פתח occurs on the יחומלך inscription[68]; note the Minoan use of פתח with ז "this" referring to the engraved monument itself, as in line 5 of the יחומלך inscription: פתחי ז "this engraved monument of mine."[69] The Eteocretan engraved stone from Psychro, as we have already pointed out (§49), opens with ΕΠΙΘΙ Ζ ΗΘΑΝΘΗ = הפתח ז יתנתי "this engraved monument I have given" (or "the engraved monument which I have given"), perpetuating the Minoan terminology; and since the scribe repeats ΕΠΙΘΙ as *i-pi-ti* in the old syllabary, we can equate Eteocretan ΕΠΙΘΙ with "Hellenistic Minoan" *(i-)pi-ti* = Bronze Age Minoan *pi-te* = Phoenician פתח.

125. Libation table I,3 (Plate X) from the Dictaean Cave contains the formula *ki-te-te-bi* . *k*[*i*]-*re-y*[*a*]-*tu*. That the final word is *qiryatu* "city" in the nominative is virtually certain; cf. Hebrew קריה, Ugaritic *qryt*. The whole phrase is possibly what would appear in Hebrew letters as כי תיטב קרית "so that the city may be well." The opening of the inscription may be restored as *re ya-sa-*[*sa-ra-mx*] = לישלם *l+yššlm* "for a votive offering."

126. The nature and variety of the Semitic vocabulary of the Linear A texts, indicate that Minoan is Northwest Semitic, and is basically the parent language of Eteocretan.[70] The words selected below are those whose meanings are fixed by context. In a number of instances, the internal evidence has (as we have seen) external support from pertinent collateral information.

u	=	ו "and"
re	=	ל "to, for"
za	=	ז "this"

[66] The Minoan expression occurs on a stone cult object as does also its Eteocretan equivalent.

[67] Donner and Röllig, *op. cit.*, III, pp. 13–14, are in doubt as to whether Phoenician פתח means "engraved monument" or "door." The Cretan evidence rules out "door" and requires the sense of "engraved monument."

[68] Donner and Röllig, *op. cit.*, text 10.

[69] The King is referring to the limestone stela on which the text is written.

[70] The Semitic population of Crete was doubtless affected by immigration and emigration between 1400 and 300 B.C. Newcomers, who must have included Arameans as well as Phoenicians/Canaanites, left their mark on the Eteocretan dialects. The tyranny of the world empires (Assyrian, Babylonian and Persian) that engulfed Aram and Canaan impelled many Northwest Semites to seek havens in the islands and on other shores of the Mediterranean between the ninth and fourth centuries B.C.

ya-ta-n(o-)	=		יתן	"he gave"
ta-nu-a-ti	=		טנאת	"I set up"
ki-re-ya-tu	=		קרית	"city"
ku-ni-su	=	*ku(n)nišu,*	כונתא	"wheat"
pi-te	=		פתח	"engraved monument"
ya-ne	=		יין, ין	"wine"
ku-ro	=		כל	"all, total"
a-ka-nu	=		אגן	"cup, bowl"
su-pu	=		סף	"jar"
qa-pà	=	*kapp-,*	כף	"pan, vessel"
ka-ro-pà	=	*karp-, krpn*		"vase"
su-pà-ra	=		ספל	"pot"

IX. NAMES IN THE MINOAN TEXTS

127. The personal names in the Minoan inscriptions reflect a highly mixed population.[71] Egyptian names, especially those ending in Re, are common; e.g., *ne-tu-ri-re* = *Ntry-r*^{c} "Re-is-divine," *ra-na-re* = *Rn-r*^{c} "Name-of-Re,"[72] *a-ra-na-re* = ^{c}'*-rn-r*^{c} "Great-is-the-name-of-Re," *pa-ya-r*^{c} = *P'y-r*^{c} "He-of-Re," *da-re* = *D*(*t*)*-r*^{c} "Hand-of-Re," *na-da-re* and *ne-da-re* = *N-d*(*t*)*-r*^{c} "Of-the-hand-of-Re" and *ya-mi-da-re* = *İmy-d*(*t*)*-r*^{c} "He-who-is-from-the-hand-of-Re."[73]

128. A few names are Hurrian, such as *su-ki-ri-te-se-ya* = *Šukri-Tešeya*[74] and *da-ku-se-né* = *Daku-šenni*.[75]

129. Though names of Anatolian and still other origins occur, the most significant group of names is Northwest Semitic because they happen to show that the cult was predominantly Canaanite/Phoenician in accordance with the principle *cuius regio eius religio*. At HT there are more offerings to *a-du* ('Addu,[76] another name of Baal[77]) than to any other deity. The Phoenician goddess Tinit appears as *ti-ni-ta*, while the Northwest Semitic sea-god ים Yammu is written *ya-mu*.

130. The Semitic name *ku-pà-nu* (גפן Gupanu) and its regular Semitic f. *ku-pà-na-tu* (var. *ku-pà-na-tu-na*) probably designate both gods and people, even as Gupanu is used both as a divine and personal name at Ugarit. The coupling of the gods Gupanu and Ugaru as Baal's pair of messengers in Ugaritic mythology, adds interest to the presence of both *ku-pà-nu* and *a-ka-ru*[78] in Minoan Crete.

131. It is hard to tell whether *da-ku-na* is a personal or divine name; in any case it is to be compared etymologically with the West Semitic Dagon (דגון), worshipped by the Philistines and Ugaritians.

[71] Homer (Odyssey 19:175–177) describes Crete as polyglot.

[72] This type of name is found in the Northwest Semitic onomasticon; e.g., *šmb*^{c}*l* "Name-of-Baal," and similarly *šmlbu*, *šmmlk* and ^{m}*šu-um-a-na-ti* (UT §19.2426).

[73] Also this type of name is attested among the Northwest Semites; e.g., *bdil* "From-the-hand-of-El" (UT §19.445). For Egyptian names, see H. Ranke, *Die Ägyptischen Personennamen* I–II, Augustin, Glückstadt, 1935–52.

[74] The main source of Hurrian names is the Nuzu (or Nuzi) tablets; see I. Gelb, P. Purves and A. MacRae, *Nuzi Personal Names*, University of Chicago Press, Chicago, 1943. *Šukri-* is common in Nuzu. Instead of *-Tešeya*, the Nuzu form is *-Tešuya*, a hypocoristicon for the storm god Tešub.

[75] This name occurs not only in Nuzu but also in Ugarit (UT §19.2526).

[76] Or Haddu, written *hd* in Ugaritic. Both הדד (1 Kings 11:14) "Hadad" and אדד (1 Kings 11:17) "Adad" occur in the Bible. The name also occurs without gemination; note הֲדֹרָם (2 Chronicles 10:18) and its variant אֲדֹרָם (2 Samuel 20:24; 1 Kings 12:18).

[77] Baal and Hadd are synonymous in Ugaritic, where they often stand parallel to each other in the poetry. For the form that the name "Baal" takes in Minoan, see §150.

[78] The Ugaritic form is "Ugaru"; see UT §5.19 for the vowel harmony that would yield the Minoan form "Agaru."

132. Kret (var. Krit, Kretan) is the eponymous hero of Crete, worshipped as a divine king. At HT he receives offerings. Men were of course named after him. The Epic of King Kret, found at Ugarit, represents him as mortal, even though he was the son of El and Asherah (the head of the pantheon and the latter's official wife). The HT forms of the name, *ki-re-tá* (כרת[79]), *ki-ri-tá* (כרית[80]) and *ki-re-ta-na* (cf. Ugaritic *Krtn*, which occurs once for Krt).

133. *Da-we-da* is דוד "David," and *pa-de* is the name borne by the Philistine king of Ekron, Padi, which appears at Ugarit as *pd* and *pdy* (corresponding to Hebrew פודה *Pôde* "Redeemer").

134. *Da-na-ne* could well be דן "Dan" with the *-an* suffix; cf. *ki-re-ta-na* alongside *ki-re-tá*.

135. Foreign names may be feminized by the Semitic suffix *-tī*. Thus HT 104 concerns three women, whose names all end in *-ti*: *da-ku-se-né-ti*, *i-du-ti-ti* and *pa-da-su-ti*. The unaugmented m. forms *da-ku-se-né* and *pa-da-su* occur in other HT tablets.

136. Whatever the meaning, the name *ma-ka-we-te* looks Semitic because the Ugaritic name *mqwṭ*, which is apparently identical, has the distinctively Semitic emphatics *q* and *ṭ*. A root *qwṭ* occurs in Arabic.

137. Other Minoan names will doubtless prove to be Semitic. Premature identifications would serve no useful purpose, but it is at least to be noted that most of the HT names are short, favoring Semitic derivations because of the Semitic tendency to limit roots to three consonants. Indo-European names, such as the Mycenaean Greek names in the Linear B texts, are often longer. It is interesting to observe that while some Minoan names persist in Linear B, no Mycenaean or other Greek names have been detected so far in the Linear A texts. Since the Linear A and B texts overlap in time, it will be no surprise if some Mycenaean names eventually turn up in the Minoan texts.

[79] See the consonantal text of Zephaniah 2:6, where כרת *krt* is the eponymous ancestor of the Cretans.

[80] After whom the נחל כרית (1 Kings 17:3, 5) "The Brook of Cherith" was named.

X. MINOAN ORTHOGRAPHY

138. The Minoan system of writing consists of signs for open syllables of the consonant+vowel type (Plate XI). Thus, for example, there are five *s*-signs: *sa, se, si, so* and *su*. The alef series (*'a, 'e, 'i, 'o, 'u*)[81] is occasionally used to indicate pure vowels, especially in the case of *'u*, which may designate the vowel *u* "and" (§121) without the glottal catch known as alef.

139. The *p*-signs cover (1) *b* as well as (2) *p*: (1) *te-te-pi* "she may thrive" = Hebrew תיט(י)ב *tyṭb*; (2) *su-pu* "jar" = סף *sp* in Ugaritic, Hebrew, etc.; *su-pà-ra* "pot" = ספל *spl* in Ugaritic, Hebrew, etc.

140. The *t*-signs cover (1) *ṭ* as well as (2) *t*: (1) *ta-nu-a-ti* "I set up (as a votive offering)" = Phoenician טנאת *ṭn't*, and the personal name *ma-ka-we-te* = Ugaritic *mqwṭ*; (2) *ya-ta-n(o-)* "he gave" = Phoenician and Ugaritic יתן *ytn*, *ki-re-ya-tu* "town" = Hebrew and Ugaritic קרית *qryt*.

141. There is a separate series of *d*-signs (distinguished from *t/ṭ*) apparently covering etymological (1) *ḏ* as well as (2) *d* as in Ugaritic and Aramaic: (1) *du* "(that) of" (cf. Arabic *ḏû*) and *a-do* "this" (m. sg.) (cf. Arabic *hâḏâ*); (2) the names *da-we-da* = Hebrew דוד *dâwîd* "David", *da-ku-na* = דגון "Dagon," *da-na-ne* = Ugaritic *ᵐda-na-nu*, *ka-du-ma-ne* = Ugaritic *qdmn*.

142. The *k*-signs cover (1) *k*, (2) *g* and (3) *q*: (1) *ku-ro* "all, total" = Hebrew כל *kl*; (2) the personal name *ku-pà-nu* = Ugaritic *ᵐgu-pa-na* and *gpn*; (3) *ki-re-ya-tu* "town" = Hebrew and Ugaritic קרית *qryt*.

143. The *r*-signs cover also *l*; thus they are pronounced with *r* in *ki-re-ya-tu* = *qiryatu* "town" and in the personal name *ki-re-tá* = Ugaritic *krt*; but with *l* in *ya-sa-sa-ra-mu* (cf. Ugaritic *š̌šlm*), *ku-ro* "all, total" = Hebrew and Ugaritic כל *kl*, *su-pà-ra* "pot" = Hebrew and Ugaritic ספל *spl*.

144. The *s*-signs cover Ugaritic (1) *s*, (2) *š̌* and (3) *ṯ*: (1) *su-pu* "jar" = Ugaritic and Hebrew סף *sp*, *su-pà-ra* = ספל *spl* (§143); (2) *ya-sa-sa-ra-mu* = Ugaritic *yš̌šlm*; (3) *ku-ni-su* "emmer wheat" = Akkadian *ku(n)nišu* = Aramaic כונתא *kunnᵉtā* (masc., showing that the root is **knṯ*).

145. Neither vocalic nor consonantal length is indicated orthographically: *a-ka-nu* "cup" = Hebrew and Aramaic אגן *'aggân*, *ku-ro* "all" (pronounced *kull-* in Semitic), the name of the sea-god *ya-mu* (pronounced *yammu*) = Ugaritic and Hebrew ים *ym*, *ku-ni-su* "emmer wheat" (**kunniṯ-*), *su-pu* "jar" (pronounced *supp-*), *te-te-pi* (pronounced *têṭeb* or *tîṭeb*).

[81] For simplicity's sake, these will be transliterated *a, e, i, o, u*.

146. The *y* of the diphthong *ay* is omitted in *ya-ne* "wine" (pronounced *yayn-*) = Hebrew יין *yyn*,[82] and *ra-re* "night (-demon)" (pronounced *layl-*) = Hebrew ליל *lyl* (cf. Ugaritic *ll* = *lêl*).[83] The *w* of the diphthong *aw* is written *u*: *ka-u-do-ni* (pronounced *kawdoni*) though the diphthong may be contracted to *ô* as in the variant *ku-do-ni* (pronounced *kôdoni*).

[82] Written ין *yn*, and pronounced *yên*, in Phoenician, Ugaritic, the Samaria ostraca, etc.

[83] At Ugarit, *Lêl* "Night" is in the pantheon (UT §19.1379). This deity's name is the base of the m. Lilis and f. Liliths who are so prominent as dangerous spirits from whom the clients seek protection in the Aramaic magic bowls. Note also ללי *lly* in the Phoenician incantation from Arslan Tash (text 27:20 in Donner and Röllig's edition) and לילית *lylyt* "Lilith" in Isaiah 34:14.

XI. MINOAN PHONETICS

147. The vowels are usually the same as in the familiar Semitic cognate forms. To illustrate this with segolates (i.e., originally monosyllabic nouns): *ya-mu* = Hebrew *yamm-* "sea(-god)", *ka-ro-pà* "vase" = Akkadian *karp-*, *ku-ro* "all, total" = *kull-* in Hebrew, Aramaic, Arabic, etc. The possible exceptions with the *su*-sign may be apparent rather than real, for this sign may have the value *si* in Linear A and not necessarily *su* as in Linear B: *su-pu* "jar" (cf. Hebrew סף *sap*, pl. ספים *sippim*), *su-pà-ra* "pot" (cf. Hebrew ספל **sipl-*, Akkadian *sapl-*); in both of these words the *si* value of the sign tallies with the Hebrew vocalization. However, it would be confusing at this stage to deviate from the generally accepted Linear B transliterations. Moreover, there is considerable vocalic interplay within Semitic; e.g., Hebrew and Aramaic *'imm-* vs. Ugaritic, Arabic and Akkadian *'umm-* "mother."

148. Initial *y-* interchanges with initial '-. Thus we find *a-sa-sa-ra-mu* as well as *ya-sa-sa-ra-mu*; and *a-ta-no* alongside *ya-ta-no* "he gave." This correlation is attested in the Phoenician causative conjugation יפעל *ypᶜl* alongside Aramaic אפעל *'pᶜl*, in Hebrew יש *yš* "there is" alongside Ugaritic *iṯ* and Aramaic אית *'yt*, and in Ugaritic-Phoenician יתן *ytn* alongside *'tn* "to give" (as in Hebrew אתנן *'etnān*, Ugaritic *itnn* "gift, pay"). Cf. also Akkadian *iprus* with West Semitic *yprs* (i.e., the absence of initial *y-* in the prefix with verbs in standard Akkadian).

149. Whether *ḏ* has shifted to *d*, whether all the sibilants have merged in *s*, whether *l* and *r* have merged into a single sound, are doubtful (§§141, 143, 144). We may be dealing in some or all of these cases with polyphony (signs with more than one phonetic value).

150. The ᶜ (ᶜayin) at least in certain combinations, shifts to *o*. Thus *aᶜ*>*ô* in: *baᶜl-*>*bôl-* (written *pu-rá*) "Baal" and *naᶜl-*>*nôl-* "sandal." The latter example is inferred from the value *no* for the sign that depicts a footed sandal (§167).

XII. MINOAN MORPHOLOGY

151. The normal Semitic case endings of triptotic nouns (nom. *-u*, acc. *-a*, gen. *-i* in the sg.) may be assumed. In any event, the nom. *-u* is present in *ku-ni-su* "emmer wheat," *ki-re-ya-tu* "town" and the names *a-du, ku-pà-nu, ku-pà-na-tu*, etc. However, some nouns (including proper names) are uninflected; thus *da-we-da* "David" is parallel to nominatives like *ku-pà-nu* suggesting that *da-we-da* is uninflected in Minoan. For the contrast between triptotic and uninflected nouns, note nom. *su-pu* "jar" with *-u* versus *su-pà-ra* "pot" and *ka-ro-pà* "vase" with *-a* which are parallel to each other in HT 31; Arabic has a number of uninflected nouns ending in *-a*.[84]

152. The suffix *-atu* indicates the fem. sg. in the nom. case; e.g., the fem. personal name *ku-pà-na-tu* (vs. masc. *ku-pà-nu*), and the fem. noun *ki-re-ya-tu* "town."

153. The fem. suffix *-(a)tī* is used to feminize personal names (especially non-Semitic ones): *pa-da-su-ti* (vs. masc. *pa-da-su*), *da-ku-se-né-ti* (vs. masc. *da-ku-se-né*), *i-du-ti-ti* (§135). Cf. Hebrew רבתי *rabbatī* "great" (fem. sg.) in Lamentations 1:1; fem. *-tī* is fairly common in Aramaic adjectives, especially in Mandaic.

154. The masc. pl. suffix with nouns (and adjectives) may possibly[85] be *-în(a)* as in Moabite, Aramaic and Arabic: *ki-de-ma-pi-na* (m. pl. designating pots of some sort), *no-?-na-mi-na* (m. pl. of *no-?-na-ma*).

155. As in Ugaritic, many personal names have the suffix *-an*. The pair *ki-re-tá* and *ki-re-ta-na* correspond to Ugaritic *krt* and *krtn*. Other Minoan names with *-an* are: *da-na-ne*="Dan"+*an*; *ka-du-ma-ne*="Cadm(os)"+*-an*; *mi-na-ne*= Mino(s)"+*-an* (cf. Ugaritic *mn* and *mnn*).

156. The relative pronoun *du* "that (of)" occurs in an incantation cup from Knossos: *a-ka-nu* [ ] *du ra-re a-do* "[this] cup of this night-demon." The meaning of *du* is fixed by the use of the cognate ד *d* in the Aramaic incantation bowls, as "is designed to foil"; that is "the cup of a demon" is the magic instrument used against the demon.[86]

[84] W. Wright, *Arabic Grammar* I, Cambridge University Press, Cambridge, 1891, §310, p. 246.

[85] It is barely possible that we are dealing with Hurrian plurals in *-(e)na* (see F. W. Bush, *A Grammar of the Hurrian Language*, University Microfilms Inc., Ann Arbor, 1964, pp. 157–162.

[86] Cf. אישפא דימא ואישפא דליויתן "the spell of (=used against) the Sea and the spell of Leviathan" (text 4:3–4 in Rossell's *Handbook*). For detailed photographs and drawings of the two Knossos magic cups, see J. Raison, "Les coupes de Cnossos avec inscriptions in Linéaire A," *Kadmos* 2, 1963, pp. 17–26.

157. *ta-nu-a-ti* = Phoenician טנאת *ṭn'ṭ* "I have set up (as a votive offering)." The *u*-vowel makes the form look like the abs. inf. (Hebrew קָטוֹל *qâṭôl*); the -*a*- may be the connecting vowel that is normal in Akkadian (e.g., *kašd-â-ta*).[87] There is a similar form in Punic: *sicorathi* [=Latin *veneror* (Platus, Poenulus 930, 950)] which has the *ô* in the second syllable and the connecting vowel -*â*- (vs. normal Hebrew זכרתי *zakartī* "I commemorate"). Minoan-Phoenician-Punic have a number of features that deviate from standard Hebrew.

158. *ya-ta-no-?* . *u-ya-*[ ] "he has given it and set [it up as a votive offering]" confronts us with the Phoenician-Ugaritic verb יתן *ytn* (vs. Hebrew נתן *ntn*). The verb to be restored is probably *ṭn'* in view of the Phoenician dedicatory formula יתן ויטנא *ytn wyṭn'* "he gave and set up (as a votive offering)". There is variant form of יתן *ytn* in Minoan, to wit, אתן *'tn* as in *a-ta-no* "he has given" (§121).

159. *te-te-pi* may be a form of יטב *yṭb*, in the purpose clause *ki-te-te-pi ki-re-ya-tu* = Hebrew כי תיטב קריה "that the city may thrive." Whether the form corresponds to the simple conjugation (Hebrew תִּיטַב *tîṭab* "she may be well") or causative conjugation (Hebrew תֵּיטֵב *têṭēb* "she may do well") has not yet been determined.

160. There is at least one shafel causative; it is nominalized to form *ya-sa-sa-ra-mu* ("votive offering"). Note that the vowel of the prefix (*ya-*) is *a* as in Ugaritic (vs. Arabic and Akkadian, which have *u* in the prefix of the causative conjugations). This one word does not necessarily mean that all Minoan causatives are shafels as in Ugaritic; even Hebrew has a shafel name of the same formation to wit, יששכר *yšškr* "Issachar."

161. The preposition "to, for" is *re*, whose vocalization goes with Arabic *li* (vs. Hebrew ל *la*): *re ya-sa-*[*sa-ra-m?*] *ki te-te-pi ki-re-ya-tu* "(this libation table is dedicated) as a votive offering [ ] so that the town may thrive" (in Hebrew letters כי תיטב קרית [לישלם). See text I,3 on Plate X.

162. The conjunction "and" is *u* (pronounced *û* as in the form of the conjunction that appears in Hebrew under certain conditions[88]; this is the form that occurs regularly in Akkadian and in Punic. It is rare in Ugaritic, where the normal form is *wa*. Note *ya-ta-no-? u ya-*[ ] "he gave it and [set it up]".

[87] Used sometimes in ע״ע and hollow verbs in Hebrew, with *â*>*ô*; e.g., סַבּוֹתָ, הֲקִימוֹתָ, etc.

[88] I.e., (1) when the word begins with a labial in an unaccented syllable, or (2) when the word begins with two consonants separated only by *šwa*.

XIII. INDEX OF MINOAN WORDS AND NAMES CITED

163. The following index enables the reader to locate all of the Minoan words and names discussed above, in Brice's edition of the Linear A texts. Texts designated by Arabic numerals are tablets from HT. Both Brice and Pugliese Carratelli use the same numbers for the HT tablets.

u "and" — I,14
a-du the god "Addu" — 85:a:1; 86:a:4; 88:1; 92:1; 95:b:1; 99:a:1; 133:1
i-du-ti-ti (f. personal name) — 104:2–3
a-ka-nu "cup, bowl" — II,2:1
a-ka-ru (divine name) — 2:1; 86:a:1, b:1
a-re (Egyptian personal name) — 29:5
a-ra-na-re (Egyptian personal name) — 1:4; cf. 47:b:1
a-sa-sa-ra-mu "votive offering" — I,4:c; I,12; I,17:c
a-ta-no "he gave" — I,16
du "(that) of" — II,2:1
da-we-da "David" — 10:a:5; 85:a:2; 93:a:7; 122:a:7
da-ku-na "Dagon" — 103:4
da-ku-se-né (Hurrian personal name) — 103:2, 4–5
da-ku-se-né-ti (feminized Hurrian personal name) — 104:1–2
da-na-ne (personal name) — 126:a:1
da-re (Egyptian personal name) — 7:a:4; 10:a:3, b:l; 85:a:5; 122:b:4
ya-mu (divine name) — 28:a:4, b:1
ya-mi-da-re (Egyptian personal name) — 122:a:4
ya-ne "wine" — II,3
ya-sa-sa-ra-mu "votive offering" — I,1:2; I,3; I,8:a; I,16
ya-sa-sa-ra-ma-na "this votive offering" — I,8:a–b
ya-ta-no "he gave" — I,14
ki "so that" — I,3; I,4:a
ka-u-do-ni (personal name) — 26:b:2–3
ku-do-ni (personal name) — 13:4; 85:a:4
ka-du-ma-ne (personal name) — 29:6
ki-de-ma-pi-na (m. pl. adj. describing pots) — 31:4
ku-ro "all" — 9:a:6 et passim
ku-ni-su "emmer wheat" — 10:a:1; 86:a:1–2, b:1–2; 95:a:3, b:3
ku-pà-nu (personal name) — 1:a:3; 3:6; 49:a:5–6; 88:3, 4; 117:a:3; 122:a:6, 7
ku-pà-na-tu (f. personal name) — 47:a:1–2; 119:3
ku-pà-na-tu-na (divine name or epithet) — I,13:b:1

ki-re-ya-tu "city" — I,3
ka-ro-pà "vase" — 31:3
ki-re-tá (personal name) — 85:b:1–2; 129:1
ki-ri-tá (personal name) — 114:a:1; 121:1
ki-re-ta-na (personal name) — 108:1; 120:4–5
ma-ka-we-te (personal name) — 87:1–2; 117:a:1
mi-na-ne (personal name) — 28:a:1–2; 117:a:1–2
na-da-re (Egyptian personal name) — 117:a:5
ne-da-re (Egyptian personal name) — 17:3; 122:a:5
ne-tu-ri-re (Egyptian personal name) — 3:5
no-x-na-ma (sg. of noun in religious texts) — I,13
no-x-na-mi-na (m. pl. of *no-x-na-ma*) — I,6
su-ki-ri-te-se-ya (Hurrian personal name) — II,7:b
su-pu "jar" — 31:2
su-pà-ra "pot" — 31:5
pa-i-to "Phaistos" — 97:a:3; 120:6; 122:a:2–3?
pa-de (personal name) — 9:a:2, b:2; 122:a:5
pa-da-su (personal name) — 20:1
pa-da-su-ti (feminized personal name) — 104:3–4
pa-ya-re (Egyptian personal name) — 8:b:4; 88:4; 117:a:5
pu-rá "Bol" (<"Baal")[89] — 28:a:3; 116:2
qa-pà a kind of ceramic "vessel" — 31:2
re "to, for, as" — I,3
ra-na-re (Egyptian personal name) — 47:b:1; 94:b:4; 62:2?
ra-re "night-demon" — II,2:1
ta-nu-a-ti "I set up as a votive offering" — I,8:a (cf. I,1:2)
ti-ni-ta the goddess "Tinit" — 27:1
te-te-pi "she may thrive" — I,3; I,4:a

[89] Receives offerings paralleling those given to the Sea god, Yamm; the pair correspond to Zeus and Poseidon. Baal is called *a-du* (cf. Ugaritic *hd*=Baal) in seven passages and is accordingly the most frequently mentioned god in the Minoan texts; see also §174 for his possible occurrence in the Phaistos Disc. It is uncertain whether *a-di* on two libation tables (I,4:a; I,5:a) designates the same god. *A-di* would be the genitive of triptotic *a-du*; whereas genitive *ha-da* in the Disc (§174) would imply that *a-du* is diptotic. One, but not both, might be right.

XIV. THE PHAISTOS DISC

164. The Phaistos Disc was found in a context of Linear A tablets and should go with Linear A linguistically. The script is related to Linear A as Egyptian Hieroglyphs are to Hieratic. The signs were pressed with dies into the wet clay, so that the process was a simple kind of printing. The signs are so pictorial that the objects they portray can often be recognized. Some of these recognizable pictographs can be identified with Linear A signs whose phonetic values are known.[90] What has emerged is that the phonetic values are derived acrophonically from the Semitic words that the pictographs portray. This means that the script was devised for the Minoan language and not for some still undeciphered tongue. It also means that we shall be able to pronounce any sign, once the pictograph has been matched with the right Semitic word. Accordingly, the reading of even the short seal inscriptions in Cretan Hieroglyphs is now a possibility.

165. The Phaistos Disc is written spirally in the tradition of magico-religious texts that starts at Knossos (II:1) and reaches its climax in the Aramaic Incantation Bowls of Sasanian Mesopotamia.

166. A peculiarity of the "font" is that all bodies and heads are in profile; none face front. The profile LIONESS head  turns out to correspond to the Linear A *ma*-sign that faces front.

167. B. Schwartz correctly identified the FLYING BIRD with the *ku*-sign, and the SANDALED FOOT (or GLOVED HAND) with the *no*-sign. The *ku*-sign derives its value acrophonically from *kudr*- which designates "vulture" or some bird of prey in Ugaritic and Syriac. The *no*-sign gets its value from *nôl*-, which corresponds to normal West Semitic *na*ᶜ*l*- "shoe," as *bôl*- to *ba*ᶜ*l*-.

168. To H. D. Ephron goes the credit for determining, on purely objective and mechanical grounds, the direction of the script from left to right,[91] so that the text begins at the center of the Disc like the magic bowls (including the Knossos text II,1).

169. There is a word that occurs thrice in the Disc; once in the simple form ; and twice with a suffix . Since the four syllable word

[90] See §§167 (*ku*, *no*), 171 (*su*), 172 (*pe*), 174 (*pu*), 175 (*pa*). A few seem to hark back to Egyptian loanwords: §§166 (*ma*: from Egyptian *m'it* "lioness"), 173 (*i*: from Egyptian *it* "barley").

[91] H. D. Ephron, "Hygieia Tharso and Iaon: The Phaistos Disk," *Harvard Studies in Classical Philology* 66, 1962, pp. 1–91 (offprint), and pl. I–IV (photographs of the Disc). Crowding of signs is always on the right of the word-groups. The left-to-right direction is corroborated by the fact that signs common to the Disc and to Linear A & B (e.g., MAN=*pu*, where the sign is consistently and often impressed in the same direction) face right. Thus Linear A & B and the Disc are in agreement as to the direction of the writing, as well as orientation of the signs.

begins with *no* and ends with *ma*, we compare *no-x-na-ma* and its pl. *no-x-na-mi-na* that occur in Minoan religious texts. The second sign, formerly read as *pi* in both of the Minoan variants, looks much like the corresponding sign in the Disc, where it depicts BREAST with the value *ha* from *haynîq* "to suckle," even as the same hieroglyph can stand for *snq* "to suckle" in Egyptian. While the Linear A *na*-sign does not look very much like the corresponding Disc sign, the latter does resemble the form of *na* in Linear B ( ), for, as is well known, the B signs are often more conservative than the A signs. The variant with the suffix, , I read as *no-ha-na-ma-ti*, which is feminine pl. as distinct from the Linear A m. pl. *no-ha-na-mi-na*. The meaning of this word is not yet clear[92]; at present I wish only to suggest the identification of *no-ha-na-ma* in the Disc with *no-x-na-ma* in Linear A.

170. A frequent word occurring five times in the Disc is written HORN+*ku*. The Semitic word for "horn" is *karn-*. However, we know from the early Eteocretan text from Praisos (§33) that the word for "town" was pronounced *kṛk* (as distinct from *kark*, which appears later). Accordingly, *kṛn-* (rather than *karn-*) would be the Minoan pronunciation of the word for "horn." HORN+*ku* should therefore be read *kṛ-ku* "town": a probable word to match its high frequency in the Disc as well as in the Praisos texts.

171. The *su*-sign unmistakably reflects the BOAT in the Disc; acrophonically this points to Hebrew *sᵉfînā* "boat."

172. The MOUTH is *pe* (cf. Linear B); *pe* is "mouth" in Hebrew.

173. The BARLEY sign is simplified to with the value *'i* in Linear A.

174. In keeping with the identifications made in §§169, 171–173, is to be read *su-pe-'i-ti* = Ugaritic *spit* "I have eaten." Now the latter is used in a magico-religious context "to eat a ceremonial meal in the house of Baal." The same expression occurs in the Disc, for *su-pe-'i-ti* is followed by CORNER-MAN-*te-ha-da*. Since "corner" is *pinnā* in Hebrew, we read CORNER as *pi/bi*. MAN in Ugaritic is written syllabically *bu-nu-šu*, so that in ascribing the value *pu/bu* to the sign, we can see the resemblance to the Linear A *pu*-sign: where the arms and legs in motion reflect the distinctive posture of the MAN as portrayed in the Disc. The *te*-sign is identified from similarity in form: a vertical line that is crossed by horizontals. Accordingly, CORNER-MAN-*te-ha-da* is to be read *pi-pu-te-ha-da*.

92 Possibly to be compared with Ugaritic *nhmmt* (with one of the *m*'s dissimilated to *n* in Minoan) "deep sleep" (specifically for incubation) from the hollow verb *n-m* "to sleep" (with *-h-* added as in Syro-Aramaic *rhṭ* "to run" and *bht* "to be ashamed" vs. Hebrew ריץ and בוש). I suspect that the Disc deals with magic and rituals including incubation. Possibly = *ha-lá-ma te-no-ma* "as soon as she falls asleep" (*ha-lá-ma* = Ugaritic *hlm* "as soon as"; *te-no-ma* = Hebrew תנום "she sleeps"). The first word is interlocked with two other good readings in the Disc: *ha-lá* = Ugaritic *hl* "behold" and *ha-lá-ha* = Ugaritic *hlh* "behold she."

Since the combination *pu-te* is a word that occurs five times in the Disc, it should be a common word, appropriate in a religious text. Ugaritic *bwt* (a variant of the more common *bt*) means "house, temple" which fits the Disc context well. In that case, *pi* is the preposition that occurs in Arabic as *bi* "in." The last two syllables of the combination are *ha-da* = the oblique case *hadda* = Ugaritic *hd* = another name of Baal. We have here a parallel to the religious rite of eating a ceremonial meal in the Shrine of Baal (cf. Ugaritic *špu ksmh bt bᶜl* in text 2 Aqht:I:32; cf. also 2 Aqht:II:21). If this is correct, the shrine connected with the Phaistos Palace is the Temple of Baal/Hadd.

175. The sign depicting the ground plan of a HOUSE ought to be connected with the Semitic word *bayt* "house" so that its phonetic value should be *ba/pa*. Since a repeated cluster begins with *pa-i-* in a context that mentions *kṛ-ku* "town," the cluster may begin with *pa-i-to* "Phaistos": as it is spelled out in both Linear A and B.

176. More work remains to be done on the Disc but it seems to be in the same Semitic language as Linear A. It shows that the Minoan script is acrophonic. Its analogues with Egyptian writing confirm what should have been evident from the orthographic convergence of *l* and *r* and from the similarity of certain signs like that for WINE: the Minoan script reflects the Egyptian system.[93]

[93] The Minoan system is closer to Egyptian syllabic orthography than to normal Egyptian spelling. See A. Gardiner, *Egyptian Grammar*, 3rd ed., Oxford University Press, London, 1957, §60, p. 52) for the basic bibliography and a brief description of syllabic orthography.

XV. MINOAN ORIGINS

177. In a personal communication, Professor Clark Hopkins points out that the Semitic identification of the Minoan language ties in with what he finds indicated by Minoan architecture. The absence of the hearth, the emphasis on light and air, and the stress on birds and flowers in the ornamentation, favor a southern origin of the palace builders. He rightly rules out Greece and Anatolia, where the winters are cold and the hearth is essential; and looks to Cyprus, the Cilician coast, and Syria not only north but even south of the Orontes, as the possible origin of the Minoans.

178. When we ask ourselves what historic factor impelled the palace builders to occupy Crete in MM I,[94] we must consider the establishment of the Middle Kingdom under Upper Egyptian leadership against the non-Egyptians who had become too strong in the Delta. We cannot understand Mediterranean antiquity until we fix in our minds that the entire East Mediterranean was permeated with Northwest Semites. The Delta was never pure Egyptian like Upper Egypt. It was "Levantine" and much of its population was Semitic. Egypt in antiquity was called "The Two Lands" for good reasons: the Delta was a very different country from Upper Egypt. Much of the Semitic population in the Delta was forced out at the end of the First Intermediate in MM I, when the palaces suddenly come into being on Crete. Who the earlier people on Crete were is another problem. But we can now answer, in broad outline, who the palace-building Minoans were, that imposed their already highly developed Bronze Age civilization on Neolithic Crete. They were Northwest Semites mainly from the Delta. However, they were essentially the same people as the other Northwest Semites in Libya, Palestine, Phoenicia, Syria, etc., so that it would be a mistake to insist that all of the early Minoans came exclusively from the Delta.

179. Greek tradition tells us that Belos and his sons Aigyptos and Danaos were from Northeast Africa but were not Egyptians; they were Phoenicians.[95] We can now understand the tradition.

[94] Doro Levi has shown that MM I rests on Neolithic strata at Phaistos, Knossos and elsewhere. Therefore EM ("Early Minoan") in the third millennium is a misnomer.

[95] As F. H. Stubbings ("The Rise of Mycenaean Civilization" = *Cambridge Ancient History* II,14, 1963, p. 12) says of Danaos: "Aeschylus is at pains to demonstrate that though he came from Egypt he was not an Egyptian."

XVI. THE DIALECTS

180. Our survey of Minoan, Eteocretan and Eteocypriote shows that we are dealing with a variety of very closely related Northwest Semitic dialects.[96] The ancient Greeks applied the name "Phoenician" to the language and the people who spoke it. In scholarly circles "Phoenician" has come to mean the kindred dialects of Byblos, Tyre, Sidon, Arvad, Cilicia, Cyprus and various outposts (including even Attica), as written in the 22-letter alphabet. The various Phoenician and Minoan-Eteocretan-Eteocypriote dialects were mutually intelligible. The close kinship of Minoan and Hebrew explains the common background of early Greek and early Israelite civilizations.

[96] This monograph is based on the primary sources. Earlier studies (including the present writer's own) have not been used as evidence. Anyone in quest of bibliography will find it exhaustively, impartially and promptly published by Emmett L. Bennett in his valuable monthly *Nestor*, University of Wisconsin, Madison, Wisconsin.

PLATES

THE AMATHUS BILINGUAL

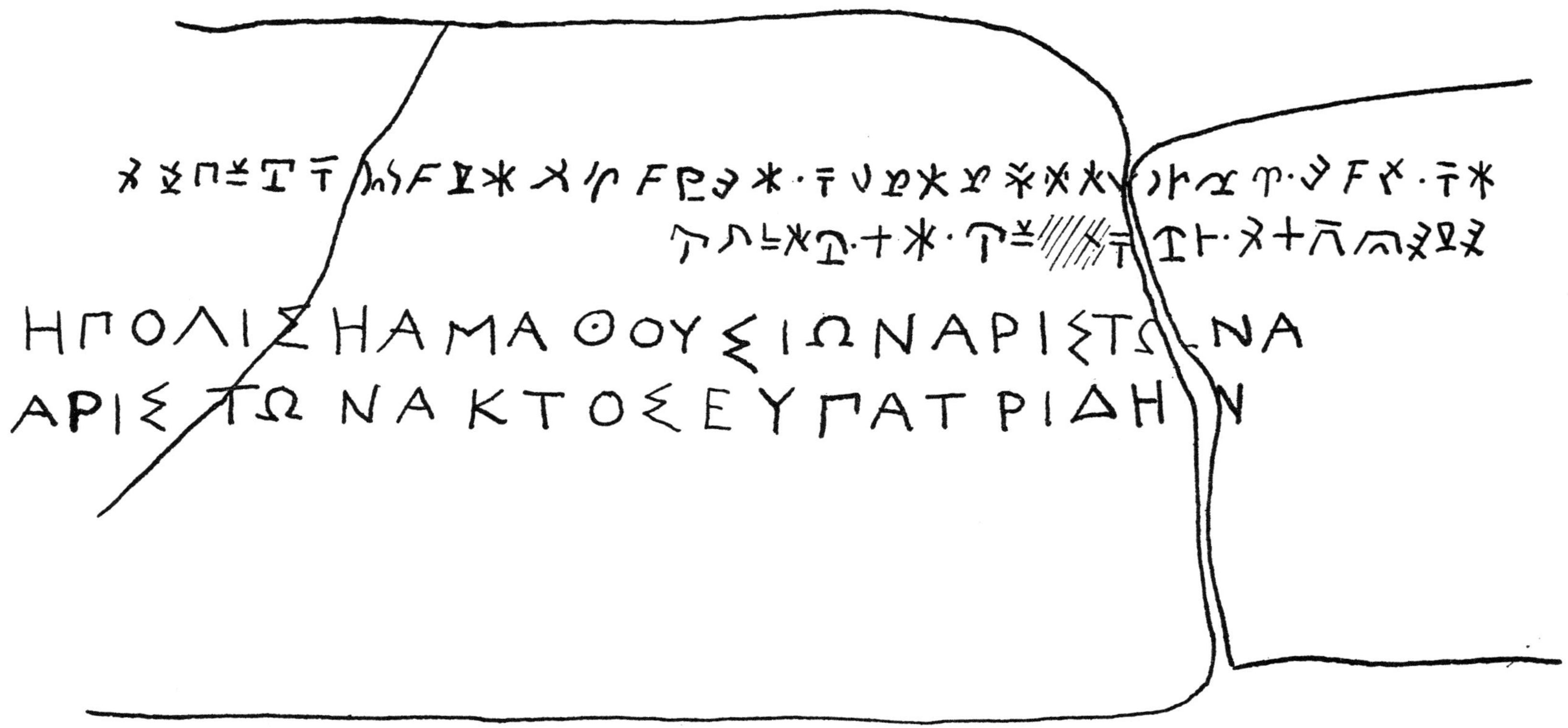

THE FIRST DREROS BILINGUAL

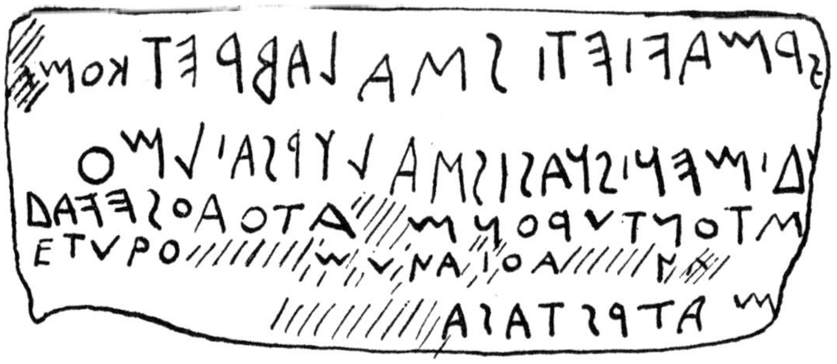

(§§20–21)

THE SECOND DREROS BILINGUAL

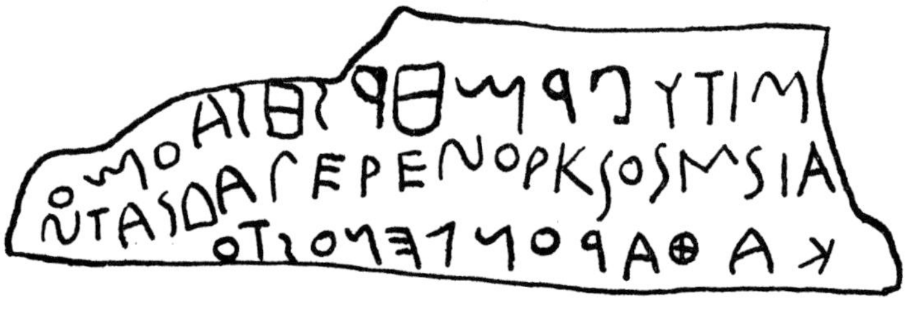

(§§28–29)

THE EARLY (FIRST) PRAISOS TEXT

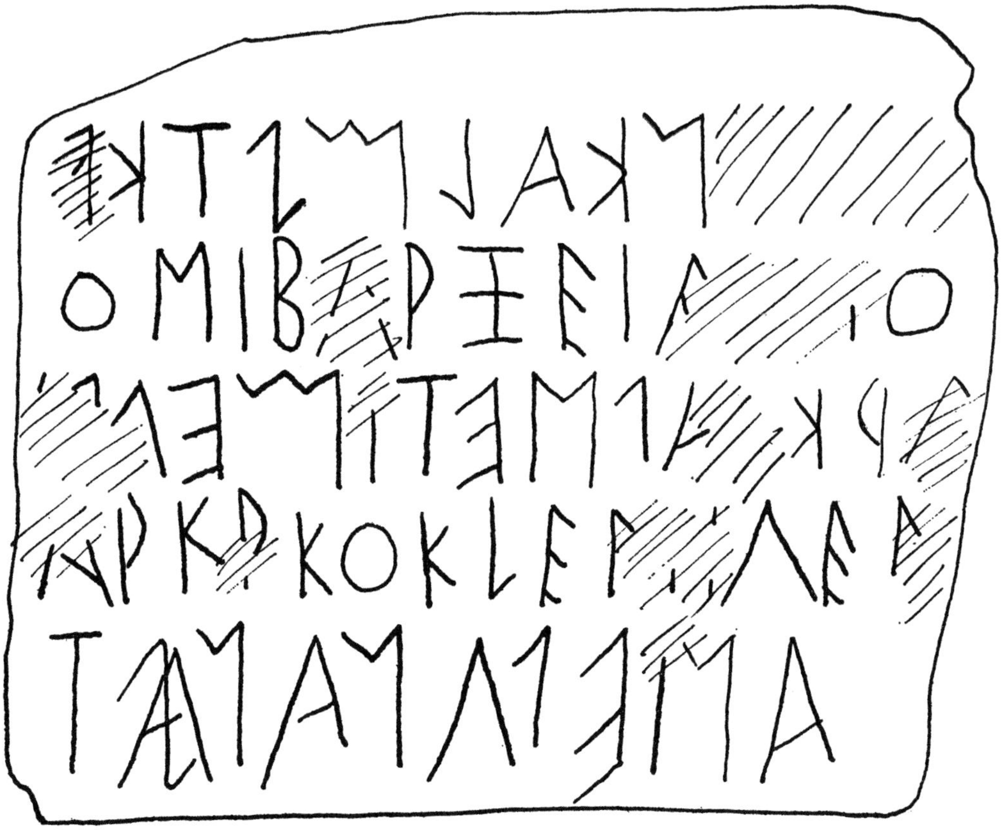

ΟΝΑΔΕΣΙΕΜΕΤΕΓΙΜΙΤΣΦΑ
ΔΟΦΙΑΡΑΛΑΟΡΑΙΣΟΙΙΝΑΙ
ΡΕΕΤΝΜΤΟΡΣΑΡΔΟΦΑΝΟ
ΣΑΤΟΙΣΣΤΕΦΣΙΑΝΥΝ
ΝΙΜΕΣΤΕΡΑΛΥΝΠΥΤΑΤ
ΙΑΝΟΜΟΣΕΥΟΣΟΦΡΑΙΣΟΝΑ
ΣΩΣΑΑΔΟΦΤΕΝ
ΜΑΓΡΑΙΝΑΙΡΕ Ρ
ΙΡΕΙΡΕΡΕΙΕ Τ
ΝΤΙΡΑΝ
ΑΣΚΕΣ

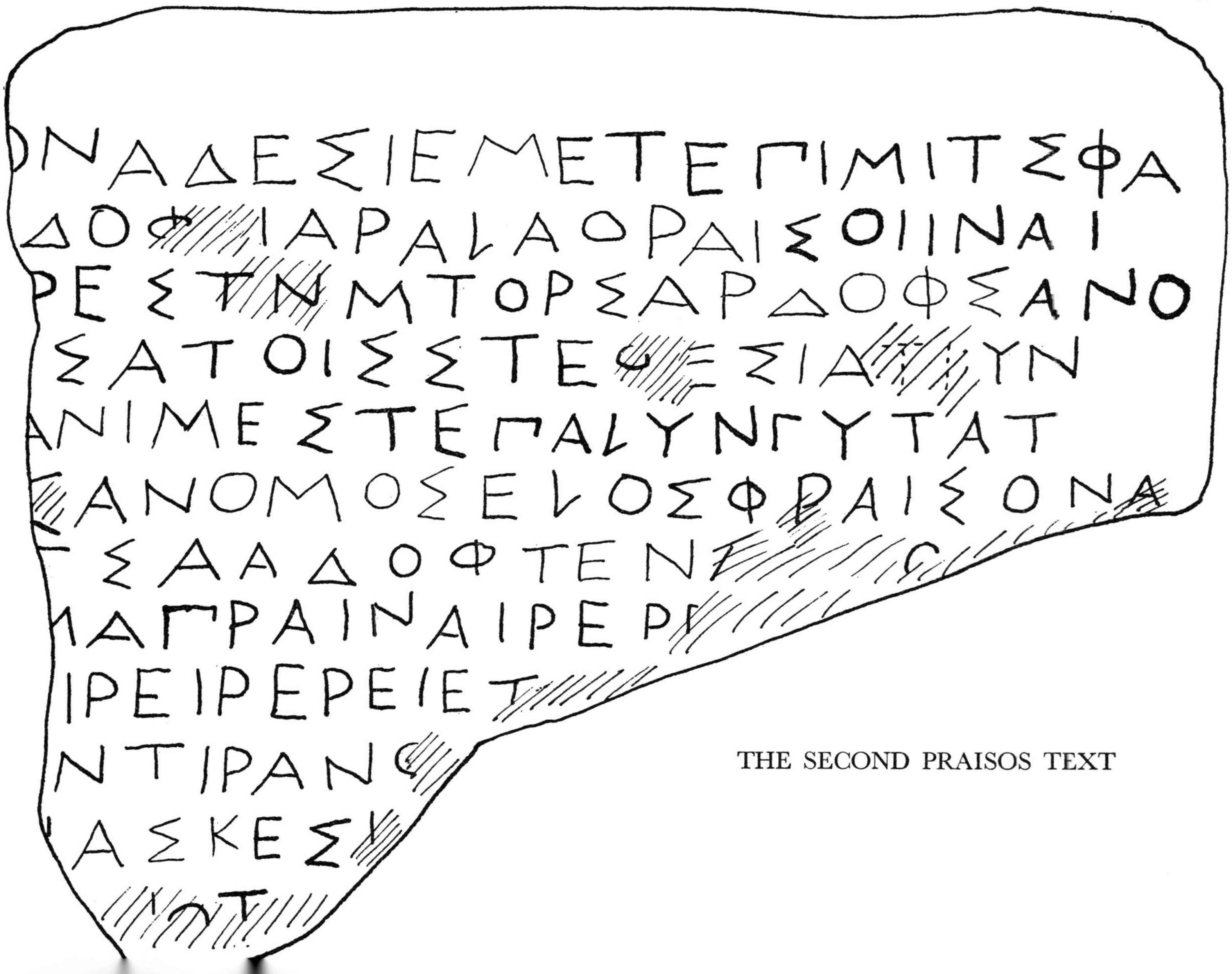

THE SECOND PRAISOS TEXT

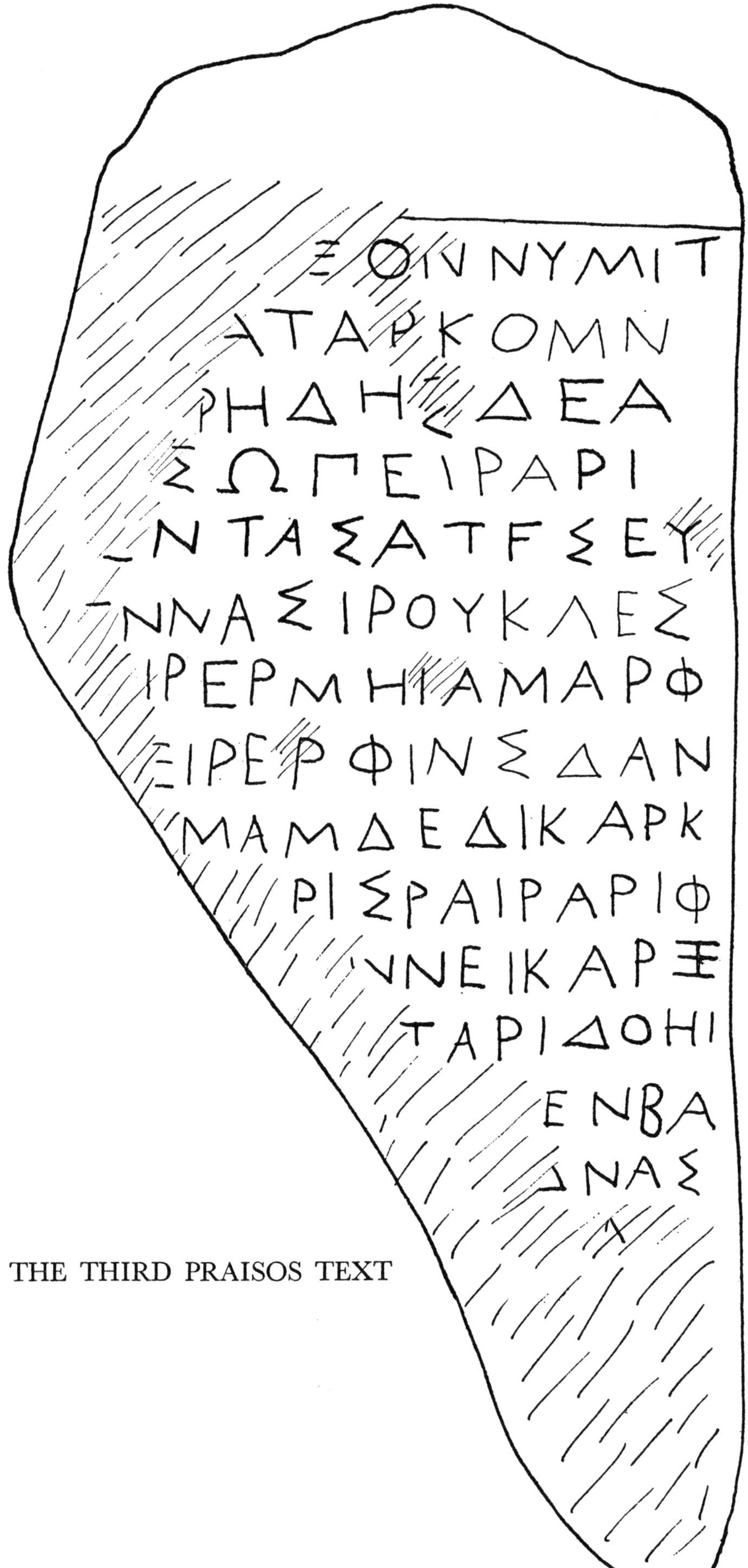

THE THIRD PRAISOS TEXT

Plate VI (§44)

THE FOURTH PRAISOS TEXT

THE PSYCHRO TEXT

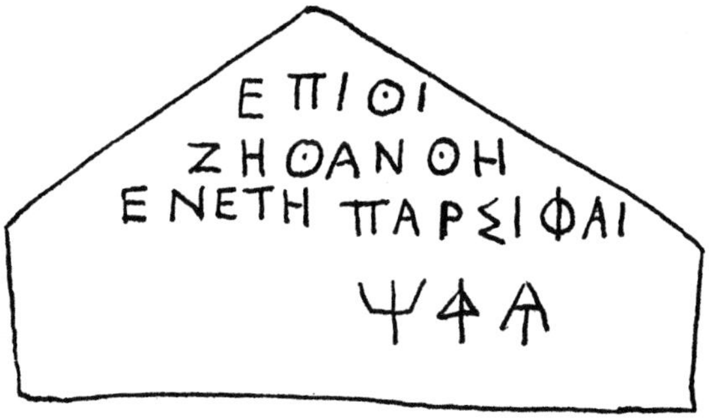

(§45)

HT 31

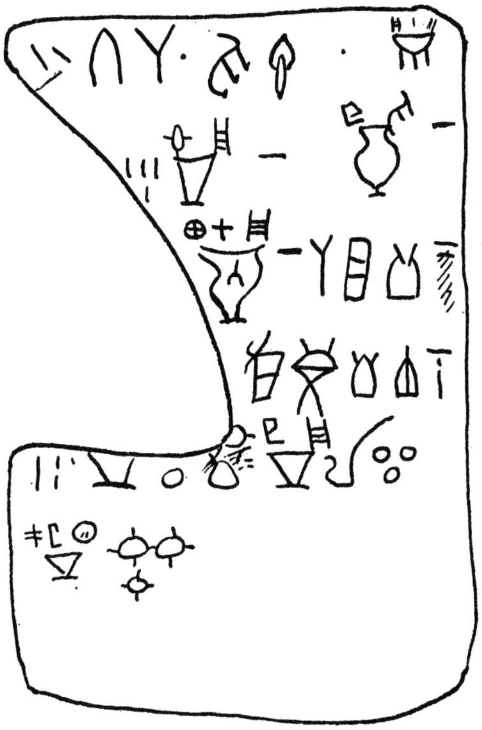

(§115)

Plate VIII

HT 86:a:1–2, b:1–2

ku-ni-su "emmer wheat"
followed by
WHEAT determinative ()

(§116)

HT 88

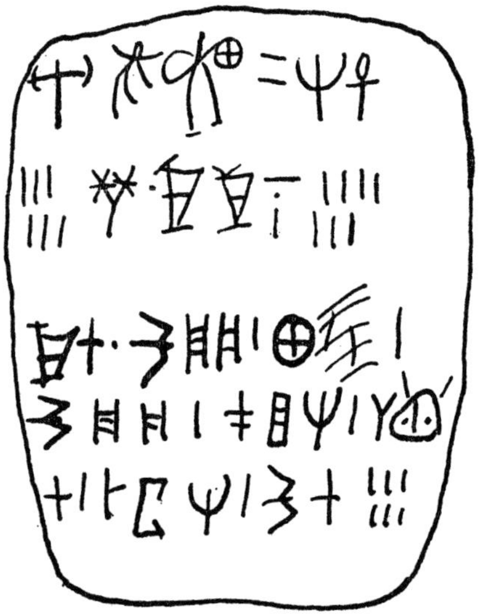

(§117)

FROM HT 122

HT 122:a:end

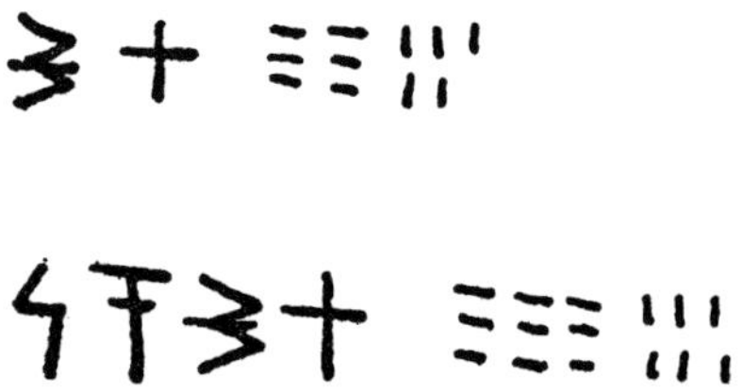

HT 122:b:end

(§118)

ON LIBATION BOWL FROM APODOULOU (I,14)

(§121)

ON MAGIC CUP FROM KNOSSOS (II,2)

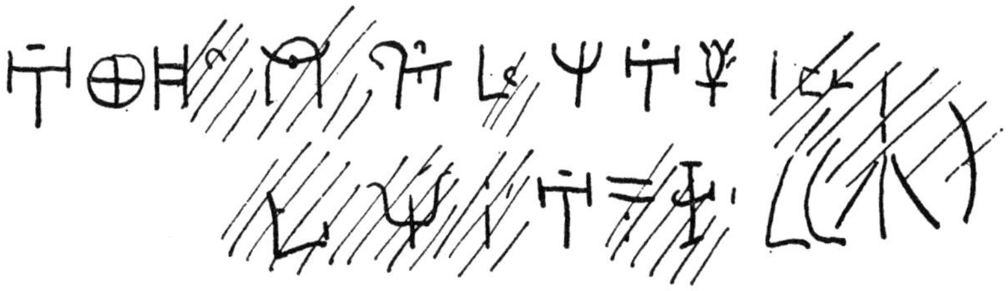

(§§119, 156)

ON LIBATION TABLE FROM KNOSSOS (I,8)

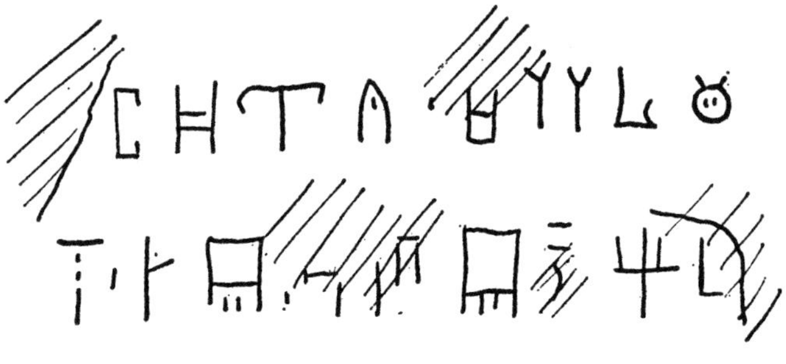

(§122)

ON WINE PITHOS FROM KNOSSOS (II,3)

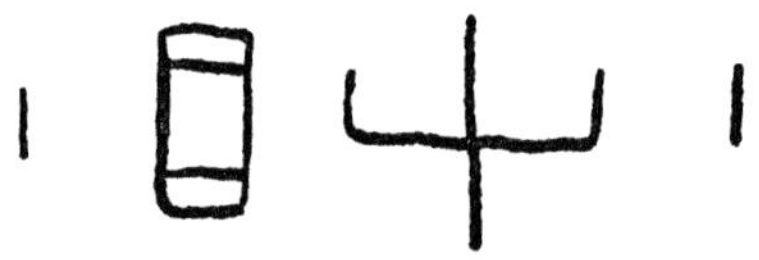

(§123)

ON LIBATION TABLE FROM PALAIKASTRO (I,3)

(§§125, 161)

PARTIAL GRID OF THE MINOAN SYLLABARY

	A	E	I	O	U
	a		i		u
P	pa pà		pi		pu (or)
T	ta tá	te	ti (or)	tȯ	tu (or)
D	da	de	di	do	du
K	ka	ke	ki (or)	ko	ku (or)
"Q"	qa	qe			
M	ma		mi		mu (or)
N	na	ne né	ni	no	nu
R	ra (or) rá	re	ri	ro	ru
S	sa	se			su
Z	za				
W	wa	we			
Y	ya				

Basis for Phaistos Disc Values

'i: Lin. A *i* & §§173, 174 & n. 90

ha: §169 & n. 92

pa: Lin. A *pa* & n. 90

pe: Lin. B *pe* & §§172, 174 & n. 90

pi: §174

pu: Lin. A *pu* & n. 90

tá: Lin. A *tá*

te: Lin. A *te* & §174 & n. 92

ti: Lin. A *ti* & §174

to: Lin. A *to* & §175

da: Lin. A *da* & §174

ko: depicts "threshing floor" with grain (=Egyptian hieroglyph "0 50")=*gōren* in Hebrew, whence *go/ko* value; related in form to *qe*-sign in Lin. A & B; see note on *se*, below

ku: Lin. A *ku* & §§167, 170 & n. 90

kṛ: §170

ma: Lin. A *ma* & §166 & nn. 90, 92

na: Lin. B *na* & §169 & n. 90

no: Lin. A *no* & §167

lá: Lin. A *rá* & n. 92

se: Lin. A *se*; the suffix *se* "this" occurs not only by itself in the Disc (cf. §90) but also 12 times in the augmented form *-ko-se* "this" as in Eteocypriote (§11)

su: Lin. A *su* & §171 & n. 90; probably pronounced *si* (§174) as in Eteocypriote (note form of *si* in Amathus Bilingual)

PROVISIONAL VALUES OF SOME PHAISTOS DISC SIGNS

	A	E	I	O	U	R̥
ʾ			ʾi 			
H	ha 					
P	pa 	pe 	pi 		pu 	
T	tá 	te 	ti 	to 		
D	da 					
K				ko 	ku 	kr̥ 
M	ma 					
N	na 			no 		
L	lá 					
S		se 			su